GARTH BROOKS

THE ANTHOLOGY | PART ONE

Produced by

**MELCHER
MEDIA**

124 West 13th Street
New York, NY 10011
www.melcher.com

10 9 8 7 6 5 4 3 2 1

Manufactured in China
Library of Congress Cataloging-in-Publication
Data available upon request.

Limited First Edition:
ISBN 978-1-59591-099-8

GARTH BROOKS

THE ANTHOLOGY | PART ONE

THE FIRST FIVE YEARS

WRITTEN BY
GARTH BROOKS
WITH WARREN ZANES

 MELCHER MEDIA    PEARL RECORDS

TABLE OF CONTENTS

Nashville, TN | Jack's Tracks Studio

LATE SUMMER, 1985.

IT'S EARLY SUNDAY MORNING in Oklahoma and we're trying to get home before the sun comes up. I'm in a truck with Matt, our drummer, and we're following the other guys in the band, Jed, Tom, and Mike, who are in the truck up ahead. We're between radio station signals, all you hear is the engine, the wheels on the highway, and the ringing in your ears from the night's gig. Matt breaks the silence. "Where do you want this to go?" I ask him what he means. "Music," he says. "How far do you want to take it?" He's asking about something I think about all the time. And I guess this is the first time I ever share openly what I'm wanting on the inside when it comes to music. "I want to be America's band," I tell him. "And I don't think that's impossible."

The band was called Sante Fe. Matt would eventually leave the group to pursue his education and writing. Troy Jones, from Shawnee, Oklahoma, would take over behind the drums. We were a cover band that played dance halls, clubs, and rodeos throughout Oklahoma . . . clubs like Norm's in Ponca City, The Bamboo Ballroom in Enid, The Tumbleweed in Stillwater, Tulsa City Limits in Tulsa, just to name a few. During the honky-tonk run, we also played rodeos. The Timed Events Championship held at The Lazy E in Guthrie and, eventually, the IFR (International Finals Rodeo) in Tulsa. It would be after the IFR that the band would

decide to head to Nashville to try to take our music to the next level.

Summer, 1987. We all moved to Hendersonville, Tennessee, five guys, two wives, one baby, a dog and a cat . . . in one house. We signed a year lease but the band broke up before the lease was through. Two of the guys moved back to Oklahoma, the other two stayed in Tennessee and went to work at Gibson Guitars. I was lucky enough to get a job managing a boot store in Rivergate, north of Nashville, for Joey Calcaterra and Cowtown Boots out of El Paso. I could hire one employee, so I hired my wife, Sandy.

Sandy and I would move to East Nashville, a little closer to the heart of things. Our landlord was Stephanie Brown. Stephanie's contribution to this thing I'll call "the Garth Brooks story," which really belongs to more people than just me, went beyond giving us a roof over our heads when we needed one. She was the person who would introduce me to Bob Doyle. Other than God himself, Bob has been the main reason this story turned out the way it did.

When I met Bob, he was working at ASCAP, a performing rights organization. ASCAP and BMI were pretty much the two places any songwriter stopped by when they moved to

Lamb Studios, Stillwater, OK, 1987 | And yes, that is Ty England. He looks like a baby, doesn't he?

"I WANT TO BE AMERICA'S BAND," I TELL HIM. "AND I DON'T THINK THAT'S IMPOSSIBLE."

- g

Nashville. Bob would eventually leave ASCAP and begin his own publishing/management company. Buddy Mondlock and myself were the first two singer-songwriters Bob would take in and take on. A moment I will never forget was when Bob and I were pulling in behind his building on 17th in his cherry-red antique pickup truck, and he said, "It's going to happen. You'll get a record deal, it's just a question of when." Hearing him say that made me relaxed and confident.

So, with demos and guitar in hand, here we went to the handful of major record labels. Eventually, all the labels said, "No thank you." When Bob hung up the phone from the last label to pass, it seemed the dream was over. Bob encouraged me to keep my chin up and reminded me this was just the first round and, besides, I had a songwriter's show-case coming up at the Bluebird for the Nashville Songwriters Association International. I told Bob I saw no reason to play the showcase now that all the labels had passed. He reminded me that we'd promised them we would be there and needed to make good on that promise.

I arrived at the Bluebird early, hoping maybe one of the performers before me would be late and I could go on in their spot and get out of there early. Though no one in that room knew

or cared, I felt everyone saw me as the guy who got passed on by every label in town. Ralph Murphy, a Canadian singer-songwriter, was slated to go on second, but Ralph couldn't make the showcase, and the producer of the show saw me sitting there and asked me to go on early. Lynn Shults from Capitol Records was there to see Ralph . . . he saw Garth Brooks LIVE instead. After the performance, Lynn approached Bob in the audience and asked, "Where did we leave the deal?" Bob could have told him Capitol passed, but he was smart enough to say, "You guys said you would get back to us." I will believe forever that answer is why we would sign a record deal the following week with the coolest record label on the planet.

I was lucky enough to have a relationship with Bryan Kennedy, a songwriter and song plugger. Bryan also happened to be one of three very talented sons of legendary producer and player Jerry Kennedy. Jerry was sweet enough to take Bob and me under his wing through the label deal process. I had always thought if I got a record deal, the records would be produced by Jerry. The minute Bob and I told Jerry we had signed with Capitol, Jerry simply said he was out, following that with a statement that led Bob and me to feel Jerry and the regime at Capitol maybe didn't see eye to eye. Jerry told me the record label would give a new artist a list of producers. He went on to say, "Bring me the list and I'll tell you who I think would be a good fit for you."

I remember sitting across from Jerry in his office as he looked over the list. He circled five names and said, "If any of these five guys will see you, I think they will get you." One of the names on that list was Allen Reynolds. Allen was the first available producer to meet with. I remember walking out of Allen's office and turning to Bob and saying, "No offense to these other producers, but if that man wants

Stillwater, OK | Dale Pierce, Ty England, and Garth in college at the Bennett Jam.

to work with me, I am fine with saying yes and getting started." Allen not only said yes, he went on to say he would produce three to five sides on me, and if the label didn't like them he would pay for them. That's the kind of man Allen Reynolds was and would continue to be.

I don't know about you, but for me things never move fast enough. There were times I would come into Bob's office and ask him if there was anything I should be doing. He would always say, "Yes, three things: *write, write, write.*" Bob sensed there would come a time when we were going to need original songs but would not have the time to write them or be in the correct headspace to write well.

So here come the songwriters, Kent Blazy, Larry Bastian, Tony Arata, Kim Williams, and DeWayne Blackwell. Stephanie Davis and Pat Alger would also enter here, but their

work wouldn't appear until the next album. Here come the guys in the studio, Chris Leuzinger, Bobby Wood, Milton Sledge, Mike Chapman, Mark Casstevens, Bruce Bouton, Rob Hajacos, Allen Reynolds, and engineer Mark Miller. The publishers and song pluggers, Bryan Kennedy, Matt Lindsay, Judy Harris, and Daniel Hill. The label staff, Jim Foglesong, Lynn Shults, and Terry Choate. I mean, damn, it was a ton of people. I never knew how big of a team it would take, and I don't think any of us had any way of knowing what was about to happen. Or how that very first record would start a ride where no matter how big the artist, the format, or even the performances would get, it would be the music that would be in the driver's seat of **THE FIRST FIVE YEARS**.

YEAR
ONE

1989

The self-titled debut album shipped 20,000 units, which was without question a modest start. The cover shot, like all of the first five albums, was photographed by Bev Parker. Virginia Team, the Art Director, hated the shadow across the face, but Bob Doyle loved it. He said it brought mystery and intrigue to a new artist. Bob always believed any long-term plan needed a starting place that left room for growth. *What did I think?* When I found out the debut album had to be my name, I really lobbied hard to name it "Randy Travis." He was selling like hotcakes!

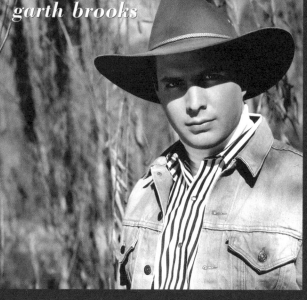

garth brooks

15

NOT COUNTING YOU

BY GARTH BROOKS

Allen Reynolds: It was late summer, 1988, and we were picking from things that Garth had written or gathered. Garth was smart in that way. He was a songwriter, but he was also an aspiring artist who was singing on demos, working a day job at a boot store, and hoping for a break. He was listening closely, and he was gathering songs along the way. Had been for years. He was ready.

G: When Allen was talking about what songs to record on the first album, he singled out three or four things that I had something to do with writing. But I didn't want too much of my stuff on there, because at that point—and this is probably true of anyone making their first album— you're just not fully confident as a writer. So I was scared that either Bob Doyle was pressuring him to do this or Allen thought he *had* to pick those because my name was on them. I was kind of hesitant.

Nashville, TN, 1988 | First promotional photo.

Remember, this town has the greatest writers on the planet. You can't out-write Nashville. But then this band took them and, all the sudden, made them very inviting, just delicious to play. Holy cow, I didn't know the songs could sound like that! These guys get it to where you go, "I want to jump in here *now*!" I never saw the power of "Not Counting You" or understood what that record would mean for us. Not until then.

Bob Doyle: Garth went in with a lot of great songs, some he'd written, some by other songwriters. When I realized Allen was choosing a lot of Garth's, I wondered if Garth was pressing him to go that way. Turns out Garth was worried that I was doing the same thing! But Allen was just drawn to Garth's songwriting from the beginning.

G: As a songwriter, you write a lot of your stuff for females. Sometimes you wonder, as a guy, "Is this too vulnerable to say?" But this one had an interesting mix. There's that line I felt really good about that goes, "When it comes to heartaches, it's better to give than to receive." When I was young, I always thought that to say you had a heartache made you a weaker person. Being the victim in a song was a hard position for me to take. But "Not Counting You" sets up that character, then it turns. It's all bravado, and then . . . damn, this guy's a wreck. I look at that lyric now and I can see the classic country style, like it's something from a Jack Greene record, or from that classic sixties stuff that my mom raised me on.

THIS TOWN HAS THE GREATEST WRITERS ON THE PLANET. YOU CAN'T OUT-WRITE NASHVILLE. - g

Allen Reynolds: Garth's got tremendous emotional range within him. He is a very emotional guy. He cries easily and unabashedly. But he's a real man's man too. He has very male energy, but has this real tenderness about it, just as he has this cheeky personality too, a great sense of humor. "Not Counting You" made room for *all* of that. It was a great way to open that record, to bring this new artist through the door.

G: I'd stand in the corner of the recording studio and I'd sing every song there. My tradition from that very first session, I don't know why, was to hold the door open as all these musicians would file past and into the control room for playback. I'd be holding the door, and I'd get to hear them making comments as they went by.

That first day, Bobby Wood's walking past me, and he—and I didn't yet know if I'd like Bobby or not, because I didn't know if he was making fun of me or not—he's saying to one of the other guys, "I haven't played some of these licks since the sixties." I didn't know what that meant. Come to find out, Bobby loved that kind of stuff. That band really made this stuff swing, and that's what I like. They're more of a Muscle Shoals kind of a rhythm section, cool and hip. They can swing the shit out of it.

So here it was. "Not Counting You" was your introduction, the first time you're meeting this guy. It became the opening of the live show. Looking back on it, I guess it was a billion times more important than I ever thought it would be when I was setting out to make the record. But it just represented the whole picture. It was the first thing you heard from us. And with that . . . we were off and running. Even if we didn't completely know it yet.

Nashville, TN, 1988 | First Fan Fair performance.

"WHEN IT COMES TO HEARTACHES, IT'S BETTER TO GIVE THAN TO RECEIVE."

I'VE GOT A GOOD THING GOING

BY LARRY BASTIAN, SANDY MAHL AND GARTH BROOKS

Chris Leuzinger: The session was at 2 p.m., and we actually cut two things in that one session, "Not Counting You" and "I've Got a Good Thing Going." Those are two good tracks to have completed in that amount of time. I think we felt like we had a pretty good day (laughs).

G: Bob Doyle introduced me to Larry Bastian, and then paid for me to fly out to Visalia, California, to write with him. It was the first time I'd ever been in a little puddle jumper, and I was scared to death. We landed out in the mountains. It was 5,000, 6,000 feet up, and I couldn't breathe, and here's Larry Bastian, this songwriter with some real credits, and he has a certain way to write a song that he lays on you once he has you out in the middle of nowhere and you're stranded there.

Larry Bastian: I love to get the songwriters out there with me.

Allen Reynolds: Larry is an interesting guy who lives on a mountain out West. He was part of a formative group of songwriters that were around Garth early on that included Kent Blazy, DeWayne Blackwell, writers associated with Bob Doyle. He's just a free spirit with an interesting sense of humor. His family were shepherds from, I want to say, Portugal or Spain.

Larry Bastian: Basque country. In Spain. Dangerous people in the mountains *(laughs)*.

G: He gets you out there and then, well, you just go on walks. No pad, no pen, no guitar. You're just walking. Larry figures, If it ain't good enough to remember, it ain't good enough. That's how we did it. His family moved out during the Dust Bowl days from Oklahoma to California, so that whole Oklahoma-California thing was big with Larry and me. "I've Got a Good Thing Going" was written out there, on one of those walks.

Bob Doyle: Well, that was, to me, really a good traditional country song. And it had that twist, the turn of the phrase. With a lot of that first album, I think Allen captured Garth in time, relative to who Garth was and *where* he was at as a performer. He didn't try to take Garth someplace that wasn't in Garth's comfort zone. Garth had come to town from Oklahoma. He wore his ropers, his jeans, and his starched shirts. He came out of the dance halls and playing music in the honky-tonks.

Nashville, TN, 1990 | Garth with Larry Bastian.

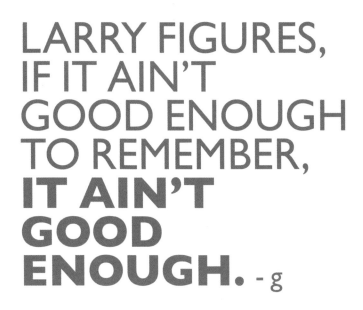

LARRY FIGURES, IF IT AIN'T GOOD ENOUGH TO REMEMBER, **IT AIN'T GOOD ENOUGH.** - g

THE MELTING POT

WE WERE IN THIS HOUSE, six of us kids with parents not much older than the oldest child, and everybody was listening to music. And being the youngest, all this good stuff funneled down to one guy. There was no distinction by type of music, by genre, it was everything. Peter, Paul, and Mary, Townes Van Zandt, Tom Rush, Belafonte, Pearl Bailey, Mahalia Jackson, Rita Coolidge, Janis Joplin, Free, Sam Cooke, Aretha Franklin, etc. Throw in Boston, Queen, Kansas, Kiss. Throw in Jack Greene, Merle Haggard, George Jones, Buck Owens, Johnny Horton. And once it did funnel down and into me, none of it could be organized in the way music is organized out there on, say, radio, you know? It was simply a matter of how much did it mean to me, how much did it resonate inside and matter to me emotionally. So, going into my musical life, I'm carrying a big bag with me, all that stuff I picked up on as a kid in this very musical house.

At the same time, there was FM radio playing. Rock radio was a big part of my life, just like country music was. And sometimes bands that were making stuff that had a country feel, like the Eagles on "Take It Easy" or Linda Ronstadt on "When Will I Be Loved," nobody thought of that as country. But I knew it was in there. Damn, I could hear it. Linda Ronstadt's version of "When Will I Be Loved" was the going-into-color, *Wizard of Oz* version of the Everly Brothers classic. If it had been the nineties, this stuff could have been on straight down the middle country radio. So it wasn't just that different formats were mixing for me because I was that youngest kid in the house, getting a little from everyone around me, it's that I was also starting to see that American music did a lot of this. Different formats were picking up on each other, borrowing and trading, and I saw that that could happen.

By the time I was in Nashville, a songwriter hoping to get a record deal, I knew that country music was my thing. I'd been deeply affected by what I heard from George Strait, Randy Travis, Ricky Skaggs, and Keith Whitley . . . all of them, because they sent this signal that classic country music was alive and well, and there was a huge audience. It was inspiring. And I know I wasn't the only one who felt it. But once I got going, the wider influences found a way in: Billy Joel, Dan Fogelberg, Bob Seger, and James Taylor—those guys were the writers. That youngest kid wasn't going to let go of anything he'd fallen in love with. So it all, in one way or another, made its way into the Garth Brooks sound.

you're the one
An worried
about

IF TOMORROW NEVER Comes

GARTH
Kent
CH

IF TOMORROW NEVER Comes
Will She Know How MUCH I loved her
DID I TRY IN Every way
To Show Her Every Day
She was my only one
"If my Time
(on Earth was)
Done)
IF TOMORROW never Comes
And She must face The world without me
Is The love I gave her in The past
GONNA Stuff Enough To Last
IF TOMORROW Never Comes

Sometimes late @ nite
I lie awake and watch her sleeping
She lost i peaceful dreams so I turn out Th light and stare off n dar
Th thought crosses my mind
If I Never wake up i Th morning
Would she ever have a doubt of th way I feel down her in my heart

I've lost loveones in The past (my life)
Who Never knew how much I loved The
Now I Live with The Regrets my True feelings
for Them never were Revealed
So I made a promise to myself
To say each day how much she means to me
To avoid That circumstance where theres
No second chance To Tell her how I feel

So Tell That some That you love
Just what you Thinkin of in case

IF TOMORROW NEVER COMES

BY KENT BLAZY AND GARTH BROOKS

Bob Doyle: So one of the first guys who had cuts that really sort of opened himself up to writing and collaborating with Garth was Kent Blazy. Kent and I had been friends as a result of me signing him up to ASCAP. But Kent had cuts and some singles and some charting songs. And they hit it off both personally and as collaborators, as writers.

G: I had passed the song to two or three different songwriters and they just didn't get it. *Nah.* So the first time I sit with Kent, he says, "What've you got?" I said, "Well I got a song nobody likes." He said, "Okay, what's it called?" I said, " 'If Tomorrow Never Comes.' "

Kent Blazy: First time I write with this guy I ask him what he'd like to work on, if he's got any ideas, and he tells me he's got something no one likes. Not what you'd expect as an opener when you're writing with a guy for the first time. But Garth knew there was something there.

Allen Reynolds: The song is just, again, one of those really emotional, tender songs, and the subject matter was something that Garth thought about a whole lot because he had lost a really good friend from college, I'm not sure how, if it was an automobile accident or what. But these thoughts were on his mind and found their place in that song. So, emotionally, the song was important to Garth.

27

G: It's about this guy who wants to make sure his wife knows that if something happens to him, that he did love her. She didn't have to wonder. And, *boom*, I start working on it with Kent, the first verse was done like that, I never even pick up a guitar. All Kent Blazy. And then that chorus lifted, oh my gosh, something was happening with this song.

Allen Reynolds: There was another song he was thinking about recording as his big ballad, one I didn't think was as good, and I discouraged it. And as it happened, I don't think we ever did record that other song. I said, "If you want a big ballad, I believe *this* is your song."

G: We get through charting it out in the studio, and Mike Chapman gets his chart, gets his bass, reaches in his wallet and pulls out his baby's picture and sticks it right there on the music stand. I look at him and go, "What are you doing?" He says, "I'm going to be right here with my baby when we cut your very first number one record, Bubba." That's what he said. What was our first number one record? "If Tomorrow Never Comes." He knew it. He knew it right after we got through writing the charts, before it was ever even recorded. I didn't have a clue.

Nashville, TN, 1990 | Garth and Kent Blazy at the Nashville Songwriter Association International (NSAI) Awards.

I WENT TO ALLEN AND SAID, **"DID GARTH WRITE THIS ONE?"** HE SAID, "YEP." I SAID, **"HOLY SHIT."**
- MARK MILLER

G 4/4 IF Tomorrow Never Comes

Acc: 154 1

V: OUT 2-5 41 1 1 52-54 14 1

2-5 41 1 1 52-54 14 1

Cho: IN RHY

4411 52-54 11:

4445 HI 6-5 6 2 5432 5 154 1

V: 2-5 41 1 1 52-54 14 1

PNO HI 2 54327 5 41 1 1 432 52-54 176 14 LOW 1...

Cho: 4411 52-54 11:

4445 LOW 6-5 6-2 5432 5 154 1

TAG: 2-5 4132- 1

1993 | Left to right: Chris Leuzinger (Electric Guitar), Garth, Bobby Wood (Piano), and Mike Chapman (Bass).

Mark Miller: When we cut "If Tomorrow Never Comes," that's when I went to Allen and said, "Did Garth write this one?" He said, "Yep." I said, "Holy shit." That's kind of where I went, "Wow, that's a great song, this is a great artist."

Chris Leuzinger: I react to the song, and when someone plays you a song like "If Tomorrow Never Comes," I mean you automatically recognize it is a great song and, you know, you want to come up with something for your part that will really rise up to the importance of the song. The beginning of it is

just so stark and sparse and there's so much space. It's just Mark Casstevens playing this lonely guitar and Garth singing. It's almost like Garth is sitting there playing the guitar on the couch with you and singing it to you.

G: We're out playing it live, and this thing is getting a huge response. So "Much Too Young" is the first single. "Not Counting You" is gonna be the second single. "If Tomorrow Never Comes," the big ballad, is going to be third. By the time "Much Too Young" has spent twenty-eight weeks on the charts, I mean

PAUL LOVELACE OVER AT CAPITOL SAID, "I COULDN'T STOP THIS FROM BEING NUMBER ONE IF I TRIED." - g

"If Tomorrow Never Comes" is getting *such* a reception live—and ballads never get a reception live—that we moved it in front of "Not Counting You." We just go for it. The second single is going to be a ballad from a new artist. The kiss of death. I remember Paul Lovelace over at Capitol, he'd been promoting the song for four weeks and he called me up and goes, "You're going to have your first number one." I said, "It's not even in the Top 40." He said, "I couldn't stop this from being number one if I tried." That was probably our first big thing, when we looked around and said, "Okay, the future is going to be yours to make what you want of it." Now let's just see what you do with it.

(Top) Yukon, OK, 1983.

(Bottom) Garth with Mike Chapman.

"SO TELL THAT SOMEONE THAT YOU LOVE JUST WHAT YOU'RE THINKING OF **IF TOMORROW NEVER COMES**"

1989 | Garth on set for the
"If Tomorrow Never Comes" video shoot.

EVERYTIME THAT IT RAINS

BY CHARLEY STEFL, TY ENGLAND AND GARTH BROOKS

(Top) Nashville, TN, 1988 | DeWayne Blackwell, Larry Bastian, and Garth perform at the Bluebird Cafe.

(Bottom) Nashville, TN, 1989 | Charley Stefl at Garth's first appearance at the Grand Ole Opry.

G: I was playing The Bluebird, and it was a scattering of people. Let's pick the number, say twelve people in there. And this guy named Charley Stefl was one of them, a sweet guy. He comes up to me with a list of people. He goes, "Hey man, I love your stuff. There's some good guys in this town. I know you're new, so here are some people you should meet." It had three or four names, one of them was Bob Doyle. Now, I already knew Bob, but the fact that this guy took that time to do that made me love him. I said, "Man, do you write?" He goes, "Yeah I write." We made an appointment to write together.

Now, Ty England was my college roommate, and we made a deal: whoever got to do this first would call the other one. So I made the call to Ty. He'd moved out here. So me and Charley and Ty are at the house one night, and I love to write about past relationships. I just do. You can draw from them. It can be one night with somebody where you just walk to the park. Never kiss them, never have sex or anything, but something in that is a seed that grows into a great story.

Allen Reynolds: There are a lot of country artists who have brought songs that are like story songs, from Marty Robbins to Johnny Cash and Jimmie Rodgers. It's always been a part of the country music thing. And I think Garth's just a really good storyteller and is able to kind of put himself in there. His voice has an authority to it, for me. Like, *Listen up, I'm going to tell you a story.* Real believable. I think that's a part of his magic, really. I liked "Everytime It Rains." It's a good story. And, yeah, it is sexual.

Bob Doyle: I'm sure a lot of people put themselves into that scenario. You know your mind doesn't forget an image.

G: This was about a past relationship in Oklahoma, and every time that it rains is when you recall this relationship. So we did the Larry Bastian trick. We sat around the house for a bit, didn't get anything. The Larry Bastian thing was to get out and walk. Here we took off around the block in the middle of the night, out in a neighborhood that wasn't that great. Me and Charley and Ty, and I told them they weren't allowed to bring a paper or anything. We just walked. It's one of the greatest memories of my life, with these two sweet guys, three of us didn't have a year of experience between us in the business, just dreaming, singing, walking, not a fear in the world. By the time we got around the block, well, around several blocks and back to the driveway, "Everytime That It Rains" was born.

Bob Doyle: I think your great country singers always had a very identifiable voice. They almost talk like they sang, when you hear Cash or you hear Buck Owens or you hear Merle. You can immediately identify them because of the sound, the voice, and *then* the story. And you believe it. Garth has that.

1991 | Left to right: Pam Lewis, Garth, Trisha Yearwood, and Bob Doyle.

AMPEX
456

GARTH BROOKS
1) ALABAMA CLAY
2) EVERY TIME THAT IT RAINS
3) THE DANCE

CTIONS, INC.

RAINS /THE DANCE

JUST DREAMING, SINGING, WALKING, **NOT A FEAR IN THE WORLD.** -g

ALABAMA CLAY

BY LARRY CORDLE AND RONNY SCAIFE

G: I'm telling you, "Alabama Clay," when I got that demo, I played the hell out of it. I was married to Sandy at the time, and Sandy would tell you, if I found a song I liked, God help everybody around, because they were going to hear it fifteen hundred times. If you don't get sick of it doing that, it's the real deal.

Bob Doyle: It's funny, there are a couple of early demos that have that theme, songs that never got recorded but were early, early songs, where you feel this bit of angst, departing home, coming here and realizing, *What have I given up to get where I am?*

Allen Reynolds: That's a song that he just loved. That motif has appeared elsewhere in country music, of people from the South migrating to the Midwest or other places for factory jobs and struggling with that— like "Detroit City" is one of the classic songs that deals with that.

Bryan Kennedy: We'd meet over at PolyGram after hours and make our way into the tape room, where they kept reel-to-reels, *hundreds* of them, wall-to-wall-to-wall. Garth and I began pulling those reel-to-reel boxes from the shelves and looking at titles. If we found a title that looked interesting, we threaded the reel and listened, and we listened and listened and threaded and threaded and threaded

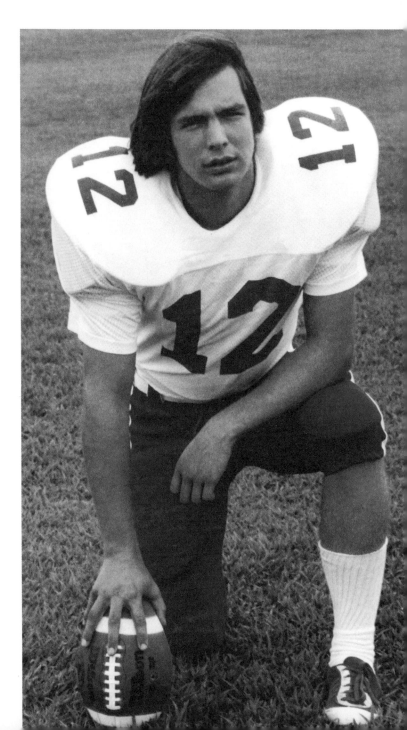

Yukon, OK, 1983 | Heading back to college.

… it was fantastic! I remember two songs Garth landed on that night: "Sometimes Silence Says It All," written by Jim Rushing, and the other song was, "Alabama Clay," written by Larry Cordle and Ronny Scaife.

G: Even the demo was a little more raucous than most traditional country. So the thing I immediately thought of was the Scholz Rockman headphone amp and the group Boston. "Alabama Clay" is the first song where Garth Brooks grew. You'd hear a lot of them afterwards, if you dig hard enough in your listening, there's that Rockman sound sitting underneath that's just the foundation. We call it the "carpet." Chris just gets that big-ass fuzz on it and here it comes. If you listen to "Alabama Clay," with all the harmonies and everything, here comes Journey, here comes Queen. What you're singing about is as country as a biscuit, but it works. As soon as you heard the lyric, just that real country thing, even if you put it in the Boston big crunch, it still is going to be country. But who was it country for? That 17-year-old country kid. That's America right there, which is who you wanted to be.

WHAT YOU'RE SINGING ABOUT **IS AS COUNTRY AS A BISCUIT,** BUT IT WORKS. -g

Bob Doyle: He's not a folk singer, but to a great extent, to me, I think he is. And I believe if you stripped it all down to Garth and the song, you'd sense some of the predecessors, a Woody Guthrie or Jimmie Rodgers type. They sang about life and sang about all aspects of it, not just "I love you, baby."

SOUNDSCAN: COUNTRY COMES OUT

Dallas, TX, 1992 | The filming of the NBC special, *This Is Garth Brooks*, at Reunion Arena

SOUNDSCAN WAS BORN right about that same time as *Ropin' the Wind*, and so now, instead of asking the seventeen-year-old kid with the long hair behind the counter what was selling, that kid who would never let the word "country" come out of his mouth, now SoundScan was telling you what people were buying. And I think in the first week there were twenty-something country acts in the top 200, which had never happened before. All of a sudden, the country music buyer came out of the closet. Between *Ropin' the Wind*, *No Fences*, and *Garth Brooks*, we had the number one, number two, and number three albums on the country charts at the same time and, I think, the number one, another in the top five, and another in the top fifteen on the pop charts at the same time. We were moving units at an unprecedented kind of steam and speed, and it caught all of us by surprise, especially me. And there's that country audience, the most loyal audience you're going to find anywhere, sitting out in plain view, like never before. It was quite a moment.

We did our first NBC special around that time, and it was the first time a network ever invested in a country artist in that way. Before that, they felt like they just didn't see a significant demographic there, none whatsoever. They couldn't pin a demographic on us. But a guy named Rick Ludwin at NBC was floored at the age difference and the diversity that was in our audience, floored at the music we were playing, floored at what he called more of a rock show we were playing, and when the special came out, tens of millions of viewers tuned in. People were seeing country in a new light, and we were lucky to be in the middle of it.

MUCH TOO YOUNG (TO FEEL THIS DAMN OLD)

BY RANDY TAYLOR AND GARTH BROOKS

G: That's Stillwater, Oklahoma. We were playing "Much Too Young" in all the clubs in Oklahoma, in the bars where you saw how people were reacting to a song. The dance floor would be packed, so it was like, *Oh, okay, the feel and the beat of this thing are right.* I don't even know if they are listening to the lyrics, but man the floor is packed. And I'm not hearing anything like it on the radio, nothing at all.

Bob Doyle: "Much Too Young" came from Oklahoma. He wrote it with one of his friends he met in college at Oklahoma State. Some of his buddies were into rodeo. These kids would get caught up in the rodeo circuit in the summertime, and some of them got caught up more than others.

G: Randy Taylor was out of Tahlequah, Oklahoma. He was pursuing his MS in Ag-Engineering, and he wanted to write a country song with one line in it, that's all he cared about. "What line is that, Randy?" "A worn-out tape of Chris LeDoux." I look at Randy Taylor, and I go, "Who's Chris LeDoux?"

Chris Leuzinger: Garth was singing a line about a worn-out tape of Chris LeDoux, and we were all like, "Who the heck is Chris LeDoux?"

G: Randy throws me in the truck, a Silverado or a Cheyenne, and we go driving around Stillwater that afternoon, listening to worn-out tapes of Chris LeDoux. That's how I got introduced. So here comes "Much Too Young." It gets written, and then when we play it, there's kind of a sixteenth note thing on the high hat and a finger roll that runs through it because banjo was the first thing I ever learned how to play.

So that finger roll's on the front, a little fiddle solo to get that lonesome kind of "Amarillo by Morning" feel of a cowboy in his truck with the sun coming up, driving all night because he's got a rodeo that day. But the hardest part came when we went to cut it with the basic five guys … the rhythm section. When the song came around, Milton took the brushes and did the train beat and Bobby played the Rhodes, and I'm going, *Oh crap, this sounds like somebody else's record.* I do my singing. We go to listen back. Everybody loves it. I'm like, *Oh shit, because these guys know what they're talking about, I don't.* I started to sweat, started to get scared. Allen looks at me and says, "I can see something's wrong." I said, "I'm just not sure we got the feel yet, you know, is it okay if we go cut it again?" We cut it again, exact same thing. So now here's the moment of truth. I'm standing there. Allen's looking

I'M THERE SCREAMING AT THE TOP OF MY LUNGS, EVERYBODY HAS THEIR HEADPHONES ON. "THAT'S IT, THAT'S IT!" - g

at me, and all these guys all at once just kind of stop and look at me, and you feel like you're in the field of dreams where all the baseball players are now looking at you and in your head you're going, *This is it, this is where you may make the biggest mistake of your life or all the sudden the Garth Brooks sound is born.*

I said, "Guys, I'm just telling you this isn't the cowboy feel that we feel at home. It's just a straight thing on the high hat, no brushes, and it's that good click that people dance to." Well, none of these guys two-step, none of them came from the honky-tonks.

They came from Muscle Shoals, they came from Memphis. But Milton hears me, starts this ticky-ticky on the high hat and Casstevens, who's the greatest finger roll player because he does ragtime, starts this wonderful thing. I'm there screaming at the top of my lungs, everybody has their headphones on. "That's it, that's it!"

MUCH TOO YOUNG TO FEEL THIS DAMN OLD

Yukon, OK, 1990 | Left to right: Leo Bailey, Randy Taylor, Garth, and Bob Doyle on Garth Brooks Day.

Bob Doyle: "Much Too Young" turned out to be our first single.

G: Randy Taylor was a farm kid who always wore the same old shit-eating hat. He goes, "You know what I want out of this thing?" I said, "What?" He says, "I just want a boat." I said, "Okay, but a boat's a lot of money, I don't know." So I call him one day and I go, "Hey Randy, you're never going to believe this, but I think this song is going to make the album." All I want is a boat.

When I called him up and said, "Randy, this is going to be the first single, I can't believe it." All I want is a boat. So we're playing The Rose in Muskogee, right down from Tahlequah, and he comes in. The first thing I notice is he's wearing a new hat. I'd known him for years. New hat. I go, "Dude, that's a new lid you got." He brings me out to the parking lot. He pulled it on the trailer on his truck, a boat called Much Too Young. All he ever wanted was a new boat. He got a lot more than that.

Allen Reynolds: I just always loved it. I think it's well written, and I loved the presentation

with Rob Hajacos's fiddle part. It's the rodeo motif, which Garth grew up with. When it came time to pick the first single for the album, he and Bob Doyle and I got together upstairs here to talk about it and that was my suggestion. We hadn't talked about it before, but we kind of all three were on the same page about it, and, for me, it presented a whole lot of who Garth Brooks is and where he came from. It let people start getting to know this Western kid. Interestingly, it was going up the charts with a bullet and was somewhere in the forties when it lost that bullet.

Bob Doyle: The single was in the forties on the charts, and the label quit on it. We had to go in and talk to them, say, "Come on, look around the country, the big stations that are still playing this thing."

G: Bob spent his own money, hired independent promotion, and got the bullet back and then went back to the label.

Bob Doyle: We were finally able to convince the label to go back after it again. That was when it got into the top ten.

Kent Blazy, Ty England,
Garth, Bob Doyle—oh, the dog's
name is Trapper :)

COWBOY BILL

BY LARRY BASTIAN AND ED BERGHOFF

Bob Doyle: When Larry played me that song, I was like, "Oh my gosh, Garth, you have to hear this."

Larry Bastian: It was about a great-uncle of mine who worked with the Texas Rangers and was in some really bad old scrapes down there. I remember him talking to us when I was a kid. I remember people saying, "Man he's just, that old guy is just telling you lies."

G: Larry Bastian, one of the greatest poets. Larry and Ed Berghoff wrote it. Larry hauls the load on every writing session I've ever been on with him. One time with Bob, Larry, and I, Bob says, "Larry has this song called 'Cowboy Bill.'" Bob asked Larry to grab a guitar, sit down, and sing it to me. Larry agreed. It's about five or six o'clock in the evening. I'm sitting on the couch. There's a kitchen door here, and the West is that way *(points)*. He sits on the couch, and right when he sits down, the light through that window comes around him, frames him with that guitar. I'm looking at him and thinking, *Did he mean to do that?* I mean, he's sitting just in the right spot and here it comes, that first line. "He told a good story and all us kids listened." I swear I'm like *(*Twilight Zone *sound effect)*. It looks like something out of a film. He sings the whole song, and I'm crying my eyes out. It's fantastic.

SOMETIMES THE SONG TELLS THE SONGWRITERS HOW IT WILL BE.
- LARRY BASTIAN

1989 | Director John Lloyd Miller and cameraman Brandt Ball on set for Garth's "If Tomorrow Never Comes" video shoot.

Allen Reynolds: The frontier and the West have been huge in the mythology of our country, and Garth grew up immersed in that. I mean, it is very much a part of the culture in Oklahoma. The song revealed a lot about Garth. And the guy he's singing about, Cowboy Bill, is the underdog.

G: It was just a tale, a story on six strings, but these guys in the studio took that and you can almost hear the prairie winds, how the saddle would creak beneath his old faded jeans. That fiddle doing that creaking sound, that wind howling. These guys killed it. Chris has to do solos, so I said, "What inspires you?" He goes, "You listen to the lyric, it's what you do." So they took "Cowboy Bill" and they painted those West Texas scenes in the lyric.

Stuck you right out in the middle of nowhere between San Antone and El Paso.

Larry Bastian: You know, his producer, when they finished that, he called me and he said, "Larry, can you shorten that song, 'Cowboy Bill'?" I said, "I tell you what, let me look at it." I did, and there was no way that you could take anything out of it. You'd take the guts out of it, and so I told him, I said, "Man, I'd love to have a single out of that song, but if you guys want to cut it that way, then you tell me what you could take out of it." I don't know if he got together with Garth or he looked at it himself, but I got a call back, and he said, "No, you're right. It's great the way it is." Sometimes the song tells the songwriters how it will be.

THE DREAM OF A SONGWRITER

Nashville, TN, 1993 | Left to right: Allen Reynolds, Lana Wood,
Connie Bradley, Garth, Kenty Blazy, and Bill Catino.

I **DIDN'T ACTUALLY COME** to Nashville to be an artist, I came to be a songwriter. That was the dream. I had that one song I'd written with Randy Taylor, "Much Too Young (To Feel This Damn Old)," and I wanted to get George Strait to cut the thing, it was that simple. Even if I can see in hindsight it wasn't actually so simple, it sure felt simple at the time, and it was enough to get me where I was meant to go. I'm guessing Nashville was, probably still is, filled with people who had some version of that same story, the only difference being the song title. What other city in this country has that connection to music?

So the people I would meet here were almost all song people, from Bob Doyle and Stephanie Brown to Allen Reynolds and all the songwriters I wrote with. They lived and breathed songs. What happened back in the day with Tin Pan Alley and at the Brill Building still happens in Nashville. Pens, paper, pianos, and guitars. Songwriters have to write, sometimes alone but mostly in co-written sessions with one or two other writers. The busiest folks are going session to session, chasing those songs down. At any moment, night or day, all over this town, songs are being written. For a young songwriter, coming into that scene is a mix of intimidation and, hell yes, pure thrill.

I don't think a songwriter has an off switch, and if he does, I don't think it ever comes back on, to tell you the truth. I think you are eating dinner with your wife, your wife is about to tell you that she is pregnant, life is about to go big, and you can't help but hear the phrasing coming out of her mouth in terms of a possible song. Or the conversation at the next table in the restaurant. You're always phrase seeking, you've got to. And the weirdest thing is, even when you're not phrase seeking, when you're really trying to take a break, that's when something's sure to come. You're not expecting it, but someone will say something, and then you'll go, *Oh, that's perfect*, and you're off writing.

When I was in college I bought my first and only book ever on songwriting, and in the foreword the author suggested that anybody that thinks songwriting is poetry put to music doesn't have the first clue about songwriting. I couldn't afford anything and I bought this book. But I threw the book in the trash. I never read another page of it, because, I'm sorry, man, I am from the album generation, and I had Dan Fogelberg lyrics posted up on my wall, James Taylor's words posted up on my wall, and they sure read like poetry to me. It was then and there that I knew already, there are no rules to songwriting. So anybody that thinks they have the rules to songwriting or the only way to write a song, those are the people that I'll probably steer the clearest from. Songs come in all forms, at all times, in all shapes and all colors.

NOBODY GETS OFF IN THIS TOWN

BY LARRY BASTIAN AND DEWAYNE BLACKWELL

DeWayne Blackwell and Garth.

Bob Doyle: That's an anthem to small towns. When Larry talks about his town, the school colors were orange and green. When you mixed them, you got brown.

Larry Bastian: Small towns are the things you run away from, the first thing you run away from and the last thing you go back to. That's a small town. You can't get away from it quick enough and you can't get back to it quick enough.

G: I love it because these guys take humor and they keep building it in this song, so they say high school colors are brown early on, but the whole thing pays off in those last lines when they say, "Hell, I'd go for a drink, but this county is dry." As if it can't get any worse, right? But another great thing about this song, the reason nobody takes offense at it, is you can tell the two writers are from a town like this. You can't be this close to the material and not be *from* there.

Larry Bastian: I live about fifty miles from Bakersfield. Wound up down in Hollywood working for Clint Eastwood and Snuff Garrett doing some stuff.

DeWayne Blackwell was working down there at the same time, and DeWayne and I really hit it off, but he was determined to wind up in Nashville. So he took off, but ran out of money about halfway there, in Kansas, I think. I sent him some money, and he told me, "Man," he says, "this is really lonesome out here, you know, nobody gets off in this town." I said, "I think that might be a song."

G: These two guys had a code between them, a promise between them of pure rhyme. If you've ever dealt with somebody who sticks with pure rhyme, it's harder than hell to write with them, because, you know, times and rhyme, that doesn't rhyme. *Time* and *rhyme* rhymes. *Find* and *time* doesn't rhyme. So here come two perfect rhyme writers, both of them with unbelievable rhythmic feel, unbelievable wit, very twisted human beings within really quiet guys. Some of the greatest lines ever, and so important to an album, because the laughing makes you not prepared for the crying that follows it. My favorite emotion, my very favorite emotion of all, you can ask my wife and she'll tell you this, is to laugh while you're crying. It's a beautiful medicine and it's beautiful to get to experience both things at once. But, also, laughter does not prepare you for the sock in the gut that hopefully you're going to get coming up after this song. Here, it was "I Know One" that followed, but it was really "The Dance" that you were setting people up for, for that finale.

THE QUOTE:

THAT'S A SMALL TOWN. YOU CAN'T GET AWAY FROM IT QUICK ENOUGH AND **YOU CAN'T GET BACK TO IT QUICK ENOUGH.**

- LARRY BASTIAN

I KNOW ONE

BY JACK CLEMENT

G: This is Allen Reynolds. Allen wants to cut this, see what the voice feels like with it, kind of a male Patsy Cline treatment of it. Very much a nod to traditional country music and a nod to a man who meant a great deal to Allen, Jack Clement, the man who built the very studio we cut all these records in.

Bob Doyle: That to me is just one of those classic old country ballads, and I think it was almost a tribute in a way. Country music had just come out of the urban cowboy thing a few years earlier. Reba McEntire broke. George Strait broke. There was a good traditional sound coming along. Randy Travis. This song connected to all that.

THAT TO ME IS JUST ONE OF THOSE CLASSIC OLD COUNTRY BALLADS, AND I THINK IT WAS ALMOST A TRIBUTE IN A WAY.
- BOB DOYLE

1991 | Left to right: Jimmy Bowen, Allen Reynolds, and Bill Catino.

Allen Reynolds: At that time, Garth did not want his name on more than five of the songs. He said, "I don't want to send the message to the songwriting community that I'm going to write everything. I'd like to hope that I can write well enough and be competitive enough to have some of my songs on my albums, but I know I'm going to need the other songwriters." Now this is pretty great wisdom from a newcomer. And he meant it, and he proved it to me, because when we had cut ten songs and decided one of them wasn't up to standards and we needed a new song, he was not going to do another song that had his name on it. Several weeks went by, and I tried other songs I could find, and finally I thought of this song. Garth's mom loved it.

"IF YOU NEED A FOOL TO FORGIVE YOU ... I KNOW ONE"

Oklahoma City, OK, Early 80s | At a club called Henson's ... I didn't have a guitar, so I borrowed my dad's Dobro.

THE DANCE

BY TONY ARATA

Tony Arata: I was playing a writer night at The Bluebird. I did "The Dance," and, afterwards, Garth was standing by the bar, and he said, "Pal, if I ever get a record deal, I'm gonna do that song." And at the time, I mean, we didn't have anything going on. Garth was selling boots, and I was loading trucks at UPS. So the thought of a record deal seemed a bit far-fetched. But he didn't think so. That ended up being the very first cut I ever got when I moved to town.

Allen Reynolds: He was at The Bluebird when Tony Arata sang "The Dance," and Garth's reaction was, *Wow, did anybody else hear what I just heard?* And afterwards, he went up to Tony and told him how much he loved it and asked if he could have a copy. But then, after getting a record deal and getting into recording, Garth was somewhat hesitant to cut it because he worried that it might be too pop.

G: I brought it in to Allen. Allen loved it. And then I got scared, kept pushing it back. Allen goes, "We're cutting 'The Dance.' " I said, "I'm afraid it's not country enough." Allen said, "You don't cut this song, it will be the biggest hit you never had."

59

Allen Reynolds: I listened to it several times and I thought, *Damn, that is so good and has so many levels of meaning.* So the next time we got back together, I asked Garth about that, and I said, "How do you feel about that song?" He said, "I like it." "Well, how much do you like it, a little or a lot?" He said, "I love it." I said, "Well if you love it, then I think we ought to cut it." I said, "Garth, go drive through the country and see how many satellite dishes are out in the yards as you drive. The people out there are well-connected. They are hearing all kinds of music, and this is a song for everybody."

G: I was at a movie theater the night before we cut that, probably four couples in there. Sandy and I were one of them. There was this part in the movie where these horses go through snow and everything goes to slow motion, and this piano riff was going on.

GARTH WAS SELLING BOOTS, AND I WAS LOADING TRUCKS AT UPS. SO THE THOUGHT OF A **RECORD DEAL SEEMED A BIT FAR-FETCHED.**
- TONY ARATA

I remembered it. Next day, I walked over to Bobby and said, "I went to this movie last night," and told him about the riff that played during that scene. He goes, "I went to the same movie." He and his wife were one of the four couples in there. "Yeah," he says, "let me play you something." Roll tape and, *boom,* that's how the song starts.

Bob Doyle: It was Allen who suggested we consider taking it to the marketplace as a single, as opposed to just leaving it and going on to the next album. If you look at it in the context of "Much Too Young," "If Tomorrow Never Comes," and "Not Counting You," "The Dance" is a very radical choice … yet it's not … but it is … a departure from what was going on, both with the marketplace and with Garth.

Chris Leuzinger: People ask me, "What's your favorite Garth song you ever played on?" And I would have to say "The Dance."

Allen Reynolds: It did just mesmerize people, and it was this beautiful, beautiful record unlike anything else, and at the concerts it went to another level with people. Garth just adored that song. So it was important for that reason, too. At some point in there, Jimmy Bowen had gone to see Garth up the road at Tennessee Tech or somewhere, Cookeville, I think. Garth was opening for the Statler Brothers, and when Jimmy came back from that concert, he had me in his car again, driving around from point to point talking about this artist. He said, "Whatever you do"—and it's a mandate I'd never had from a record label—"Whatever you do on this next record, just get me as much of that guy that I saw on stage onto the record as you possibly can." Which was great. It was like, "Don't hold back, don't be conservative." It was wonderful. The show that Bowen saw Garth on, Garth got a standing ovation, and Bowen pointed out to me that the standing ovation started in the back, not because the front rows were standing up and causing the audience to go, "Oh," and then get up. It was like a swell from the back. Jimmy said to me that day, "This kid is a natural, and you're lucky if you know a natural in your whole lifetime."

application for employment

Cowtown Boot Co., Inc., is an equal opportunity employer which follows a policy of non-discrimination in employment on any basis, including race, creed, color, age, sex, religion or national origin.

_SL_

PERSONAL INFORMATION: Date _May 29_ 19_87_ SSN

Name _Brooks_   _Troyal_   _Garth_
     Last   First   Middle

Address _104 Forrest Meadows Court_   _Hendersonville_ _TN._ _37075_
       Street   City   State   Zip

Phone (_615_) _822-5341_ Marital Status _Married_ Height _6'1"_ Weight _205_

Own Home? _____ Rent Home? _X_ Rent Apartment? _____

Date of Birth _2/7/62_   Place of Birth _Tulsa, Oklahoma_

Name of relatives employed by Cowtown Boot Co., Inc. _None_

EMPLOYMENT DESIRED:

Position _Sales Clerk_ Date You Can Start _As Soon As possible_ Salary Desired _—_

Are you employed now? _No_ Where? _—_

How long? _—_ May we inquire of your present employer? _Yes – my old employer_

EDUCATION:

Name/Location of Grammar School _Myres / Yukon, Oklahoma_ Graduate? _Yes_

Name/Location of High School _Yukon / Yukon High School_ Graduate? _Yes_

Name/Location of College _Okla. State Univ./Stillwater, OK._ Years Completed _4 yrs_

Trade or Business School _—_ Courses completed _—_

Subjects of Special Study or Graduate Work _Graduate work on Marketing_

What foreign languages do you speak? _None_ Read? _—_ Write? _—_

EMPLOYMENT HISTORY: (List last four employers, starting with most recent.)

From _Aug 85_ to _May 87_: _Dupree Sports Equipment_ Position _Sales Clerk_

From _Aug 81_ to _Aug 85_: _OSU Alumni Association_ Position _Recruiter_

From _Summer 79_ to _Fall 81_: _Kings & Mazzio Pizza_ Position _Waiter_

From _Summer 76_ to _Summer 89_: _City Worker_ Position _Laborer_

_1-800-492-6900_

_00050_

COMPLETE AND SIGN ON OTHER SIDE

YEAR TWO

1990

This album cover was shot in beautiful, rich, gradating colors. But like the first, the idea was to continue the sense of mystery around who the artist was at the time. So, one roll of black-and-white film was shot, creating a darker album cover that didn't reveal too much about what the artist looked like, who he was.

Bob wanted listeners to focus on what the music sounded like, to be in that world. I picked the album title *No Fences* because once you hear "The Thunder Rolls" into "New Way To Fly"…"Friends In Low Places," "Mr. Blue," "Unanswered Prayers," "Wolves," it just became clear that this record had no boundaries, and, as much as we could guess, the future was whatever the music wanted it to be. We were beginning to feel that, really, there were no fences and we'd be fools to put any up.

garth brooks

NO FENCES

1990 | IT WAS A YEAR OF FIRSTS.
The first nationwide club tour, the first time ever on radio, and, speaking of radio, my first Country Radio Seminar, where I would meet songwriter Victoria Shaw. This was also around the time I would get to see more of another writer, Jenny Yates. Though both writers' collaborations wouldn't show up until later albums, their writing would have a strong impact on my career and on me as a person and an artist. And when you're talking about impact, *No Fences* would be the first time Trisha Yearwood would lend her voice to the music. Some very, very important people were coming into the mix.

A lot of *No Fences* was written at the same time as the first album, so there was no "sophomore jinx" feeling among us. The original Garth Brooks album and the *No Fences* album were more like Part One and Part Two of a debut. As a last track on Part One, "The Dance" was a massive song for us, not necessarily in sales, but in the fact that it put us in our own light. Not above or ahead of anyone, just in our own space. And when the people give you that spotlight, what you deliver next will determine the rest of your career. And what came next? A song called "Friends in Low Places." Part One led into Part Two in a way that just couldn't have worked better.

I'd say the success of Garth Brooks also gave us the confidence to go ahead and make some musical moves that were a little more bold. You could take that Rockman underneath "Alabama Clay" and bring it out

a little more in a song like "Victim of the Game," where it sounds more like the Eagles than it does something from Garth Brooks. These were choices that, at least at that time in country music, were really significant, you know, bringing in elements from this other format, the classic 1970s and 1980s rock.

That's why *No Fences* was called *No Fences*, because the music was pushing out. You couldn't put it in a box. "The Thunder Rolls" threw everybody for a loop, but then "New Way to Fly" brings you right back to that Merle Haggard influence.

We were taking it to new places but maintaining contact with home. It was the music itself, and the success of the debut, that gave us this idea that we were working with "no fences" to hold us back. I'm sure every young artist has that experience where an industry wants to put a stamp on your forehead, because then they know how to handle you, know what to do with you. But when it came to this record, you couldn't figure out where it was coming from and where it was going.

All you knew was, *Man, there's something about this record that makes me pull for it. Something about it that makes me want to hear it again.* I just know that's how it hit me.

THE THUNDER ROLLS

BY PAT ALGER AND GARTH BROOKS

Garth and Pat Alger.

Pat Alger: This town is full of songwriters. I mean, I used to have guys come by to fix things on my house and see a guitar and go, "Hey, are you a songwriter?" I'd go, "Yeah," and they'd go, "Yeah, me too, I had a cut on George Jones a couple years ago." You'd be going, *Shit, I'm not only competing with pros, I'm competing with the HVAC guy.*

G: We write this one about the time of the first album, but we're not going to cut it for *Garth Brooks*, because *Garth Brooks* is way too innocent, just way too innocent of a project. So we have these songs like "The Thunder Rolls" and "Friends in Low Places" for quite a long time. Now it's early summer 1990, a year and a half from when the *Garth Brooks* album comes to when *No Fences* is released.

Pat Alger: I knew Allen, had a couple number one records with Kathy Mattea. So I was over at his place one day, coming out of the administration office that was right across the hall from Allen's, and he was coming out of his office at the same time and had this guy with him in a duster and cowboy hat. I'm thinking, *Hmm, Allen's working with John Wayne, I didn't know that.* He really looked like a cowboy. But Allen stopped me and said, "I want to introduce you to Garth." Then, after Garth left, he says, "You know, he's a pretty good writer, you might want to get together with him."

HE'S STILL JUST GARTH. HE DOESN'T HAVE A RECORD OUT YET, SO **WE WERE ACTUALLY TRYING TO GET SOMEBODY ELSE TO CUT THESE SONGS.**
- PAT ALGER

G: In that time before the first album comes, I'm scared. I need to get songs cut by other people as a writer.

Pat Alger: It turned out that night Garth was playing at a little club downtown that was a real seedy place. I wasn't that anxious about going down there, but I ended up going anyway. There were about thirty or forty people in there, all tourists probably, and he stood up there and he sang "If Tomorrow Never Comes," "Much Too Young," and some other stuff, and he had these guys in the palm of his hand just like he had a big record out. I went, *Whoa, this guy's got something.* So we talked after the show and made an appointment to write some songs.

G: Writing with Pat is a blessing and a curse … The blessing is he can carry the session, his choices of tempo, chord changes, and lyric rival the best in the songwriting world. The curse is he rivals the best in the songwriting world, and you don't want to be deadweight. You learn early, if you are going to a songwriting session, *bring ideas with you.*

Pat Alger: The second time we got together, we wrote "The Thunder Rolls." He came in with this idea that somebody would be cheating on somebody, and anytime something happened between them the thunder would be rolling. I go, "Yeah, I get it, so the thunder is playing something like the part of the Greek chorus." I see the idea, and we get the song. Of course, he's still just Garth. He doesn't have a record out yet, so we were actually trying to get somebody *else* to cut these songs we were writing.

G: We pitched "The Thunder Rolls." Allen doesn't know this. Pat calls me and says, "Hey, Jerry Crutchfield wants to talk about 'The Thunder Rolls' for Tanya Tucker." I said, "Great." So we go, and this was the first time ever in a record building for me. It was pretty cool. I walk in there, gold records everywhere. Jerry Crutchfield tells us he really likes the song, but

I WAS PROBABLY AT SEVENTY, SEVENTY-FIVE MILES PER HOUR ON MUSIC ROW, AND YOU NEVER GET TO DO THAT, WITH THAT SONG JUST PLAYING AT TOP VOLUME. - g

goes, "I want to know what happened in this song, I think there's another verse here." So me and Pat added a verse, wrote the song to where you couldn't tell if she killed him or killed herself, but it was a little more conclusive. And we were proud of it, man, loved it. But Allen didn't like that last verse.

Allen Reynolds: That song was written upstairs by Garth and Pat Alger, and before I knew what was happening, they had given it away to Tanya Tucker, and I came to understand that Jerry Crutchfield, who produced her, wanted a third verse. So they wrote this third verse for it, and at some point I got a chance to say to Garth, "Why are you giving these things away? Why are you not keeping that song for yourself?" And he just went, "Oh." It was just the songwriter in him, like, *Gosh, a Tanya Tucker cut.*

G: Allen didn't like somebody pulling down a record to hear somebody die in the last verse. But he still wanted the song, just without the new verse. As it happened, Jimmy Bowen at Capitol scratches the Tanya Tucker project. So the song "The Thunder Rolls" comes back to us. Perfect timing. We cut "The Thunder Rolls" without the last verse.

Allen Reynolds: Thank God, we got it back. That track came together pretty quickly here. The band just understood the dynamic of that song really well, you know. The things that Chris played on the slide guitar, it all just went so far to create the mood of that song. It was just charmed. And then Garth asked if we could add the thunder. I had some thunder sound effects left over from the Memphis Boys project that hadn't been used. The day we were adding that, Garth was here, and we had put it all on a two-track tape so that we could dub it over to the multitrack, and we put Garth in charge of starting the tape. We thought we'd need to edit this in, fit the thunder in the spots we needed it. But when he pressed play and, without us doing anything, the sounds lined up with the track, and I mean perfectly. We all sat there going like, *Whoa*, because everything was happening right where it was supposed to. One of those moments.

Pat Alger: One of the things you learn when you're here for a while as a songwriter is you should just go on to the next day, write the next song. Don't wait and watch. And that's what I did. I just went on to the next thing. The only thing I *did* watch was when the first album came out. We had all these great songs I'd written with Garth and none of them were on there, and I kind of went, *Fuck. Damn.* I mean, I was really kind of, what would you call it? Mostly disappointed. But I just wasn't smart enough to know what Garth knew, that he was going to need some really great songs to follow that first album, and he held them back.

G: We'd just got our very first new car we'd ever got, still living in a rental house. I did a commercial for a place up in Kentucky, and they gave us a demo model of this car for Sandy. A little Mitsubishi Starion, a two-seater turbo. I'd never had a fast car in my life. I remember getting the rough mix of "The Thunder Rolls" after cutting it that night, getting it on a cassette, putting it in the car and pulling out, it was probably two o'clock in the morning, all mist. I looked down Music Row and it was all just blinking yellow lights. I bet you I was probably at seventy, seventy-five miles per hour on Music Row, and you never get to do that, with that song just playing at top volume. I don't think there was any question about how we were going to kick off the sophomore record.

Nashville, TN, 1989 | Fan Fair.

NEW WAY TO FLY

BY KIM WILLIAMS AND GARTH BROOKS

G: I saw several songs come through with Kim Williams's name on them. I'm thinking, *Damn, this writer is amazing. I need to know this woman, I need to write with her.* So I call, and the guy I talk to on the phone, he says, "Let me tell you a little bit about Kim." I said, "Okay." He says, "Well, he looks …" I said, "*Wait*, wait, wait a minute. Did you say *he?* Kim's a guy?" I've never met a guy Kim. My heart's broken already. Now I'm trying to find a way to get out of the session.

The guy on the phone says, "He's been in an accident, an explosion. His face has been burned." I'm like, "Okay, well, let's go ahead and set this session up." Five minutes after you meet this guy, you don't even notice it anymore. He's such a sweetheart. Loud? Oh my God, he's loud. He doesn't mean to be. He's

1993 | Left to right: Kent Blazy, Garth, and Kim Williams.

loud, he's funny. He's serious, and he's an unbelievable talent. Missing a finger from the explosion. We were sitting there talking, when the conversation turned to a country artist who was dating a movie actress. When I asked Kim what he thought about her dating him, he replied, "Hell! I'm better-looking than that guy, and I've been on fire!" Makes you love him, don't it? *(laughs)*

Bob Doyle: Kim Williams came over to the office to write, and he knows I'm a pilot, and we start talking about flying and then, for whatever reason, it leads to birds. He says, "You ever see those birds as you come around Interstate 65 up there on those high wires?" And I said, "Yeah." And later that day, they wrote "New Way to Fly."

G: So we're writing in his little place over here between 17th and 18th. Cockroaches everywhere. He's rented this little apartment. He talks about coming in from Knoxville, seeing these birds up on the high line, and says, "I love that imagery." I said, "Sounds great." He started it. I said, "*Oh*, you're talking Haggard now." That nice big stroke that Haggard did on

Trisha Yearwood: I just remember being blown away by the song, immediately. I couldn't wait to sing on it, I couldn't wait to put that Bonnie Owens high harmony on it like she did on all those Haggard records.

Allen Reynolds: "The Thunder Rolls" and "New Way to Fly," they just felt so good together. My method of sequencing was, after we had all the sides finished, to tear up ten little pieces of paper and write the titles on them, and then just start arranging them and trying different sequence arrangements, and it usually fell together pretty naturally. They would almost sequence themselves sometimes.

NO QUESTION IT'S COUNTRY.
- g

G: I remember sitting in the alley with Kim Williams around the time of the first record, because he was a new writer at the time. I said, "Kim, I hate to tell you this, it's not going to make the record. It just isn't. We've got too many ballads." And his face just sank. I said, "But I want to tell you, we're working on this new album called *No Fences*, and I think it's going to be on there." And he was good about it.

all those things like "My Favorite Memory," and I'm like, "Yes, my God, okay let's write it for Haggard." And we sat down and wrote a Haggard song. On the record I'm doing my best Merle Haggard impersonation that I can on that vocal, that Allen will let me, you know. And then that whole *(sings)* "New Way to Fly …," there's the whole big three-part harmony, that sting that Haggard would get on records like "Tonight the Bottle Let Me Down." That number two spot on an album is so important, and this just fit right there. No question it's country.

He's told this story many times. He took it well, he looked at me and said, "Thanks." When what he really wanted to do was roll his eyes and say … "Oh, great." *(laughs)*

TWO OF A KIND, WORKIN' ON A FULL HOUSE

BY BOBBY BOYD, WARREN HAYNES AND DENNIS ROBBINS

Kent Blazy: I love that Garth would do songs like "Two of Kind, Workin' on a Full House." You know, about a married couple. Actually happy.

Bob Doyle: I remember we found that on a tape at the office, because another guy had recorded it as an artist demo. He was trying to get a deal, but we heard that song and it's almost like, this was Garth Brooks.

G: A guy named John Northrup, this cowboy—and I mean, you're talking about *cowboy*—he had these demos and that was where I heard it. He was going for a record deal. There's John Northrup singing "Two of a Kind, Workin' on a Full House," and I said, "John, congratulations, that song right there is a freaking hit, but I'm going to ask you this: if you don't get your record deal, I'd love for you to let me know, because that song's huge." And he goes, "I will, I'll let you know." So he's a cowboy, and we define cowboys as men of their word. The day he lost his record deal, and I mean it was *the* day, I would have waited a week because I'd have been so fucking pissed and in denial, but the day he lost it, he called me. He said, "Man, I just got turned down from a record deal." He says, "If you want that song, it's yours." We cut it immediately, because we didn't want anybody else getting a hold on it or anything.

Allen Reynolds: I remember after this album came out being out in Murfreesboro at Middle Tennessee State, where Garth had done a concert, and a whole lot of Nashville, Nashville music industry, went out to see him because he was happening and new to them still. Afterwards, I was walking across the campus back to my car, and I remember this group of girls somewhere behind me walking along, happy as they could be after the concert, singing, "Two of a Kind, Workin' on a Full House" at the top of their lungs, and smiling to myself, thinking, *Yeah, it does feel that good.*

Chris Leuzinger: The thing that hits me listening to this is Garth, just his ability, like going from "The Thunder Rolls" to this song, vocally. It's like the other side of the world, but he is equally believable and equally great at singing both.

G: I don't know what it is, because it's classic country, timeless. The beat, I guess. But I swear, more than any other song, when you are going to publishers for a record, the first thing they say is, Is there going to be a "Two of a Kind" on this record? It seems to be a pretty simple, straightforward beat, but finding something with that kind of feel … it's eluded me for twenty years afterward.

WE CUT IT IMMEDIATELY, BECAUSE WE DIDN'T WANT ANYBODY ELSE GETTING A HOLD ON IT. - g

VICTIM OF THE GAME

BY MARK D. SANDERS AND GARTH BROOKS

It took a little time but I guess you finally learned –
Promises get broken, bridges do get burned
You've been sifting through the ashes
Searching for the flame
Holding on to nothing   like a victim of the game

You were standing way to close to see it fall apart
And they're were things you couldn't hear cause you were listening with your heart
You can't say I didn't warn you – there's no one else to blame
Your the last to know that your a victim of the game

It don't matter who you are it never asks your name
All you need is a heart to be a victim of the game

A VICTIM OF THE GAME

IT TOOK A LITTLE TIME BUT I GUESS YOU FINALLY LEARNED
PROMISES GET BROKEN BRIDGES DO GET BURNED
YOU'VE BEEN SIFTIN' THROUGH THE ASHES SEARCHIN' FOR THE FLAME
HOLDIN' ON TO NOTHING LIKE A VICTIM OF THE GAME

YOU WERE STANDIN' WAY TOO CLOSE TO SEE IT FALL APART
THERE WERE WORDS YOU COULDN'T HEAR LISTENIN' WITH YOUR HEART
YOU CAN'T SAY I DIDN'T WARN YOU THERE'S NO ONE ELSE TO BLAME
YOU'RE JUST THE LAST TO KNOW THAT YOU'RE A VICTIM OF THE GAME

IT DON'T MATTER WHO YOU ARE
IT TREATS EVERYONE THE SAME
ALL YOU NEED IS A HEART
TO BE A VICTIM OF THE GAME

When I look into your eyes I can feel the pain
NOW I SEE YOU IN THE MIRROR AND I SWEAR YOU LOOK THE SAME
BUT I CAN'T AVOID THE EYES OF A VICTIM OF THE GAME
Staring in the mirror at a victim of the game
WHEN I SEE YOU IN THE MIRROR I WANNA LOOK THE OTHER WAY

But there's no one quite as blind

BY: MARK D SANDERS
COWBOY GARTH BROOKS

Ya know it's really getting to ya when ya take to telling lies
Ya can try to fool your friends but ya can't look 'em in the eyes
There ain't no standing tall in the shame of the shame
Cause everybody knows that your a victim of the game
When

Chris Leuzinger: We cut "Unanswered Prayers" and "Wild Horses" in the afternoon. In the evening, "The Thunder Rolls" and "Victim of the Game."

G: "Victim of the Game," that thing is solid. You can jump up and down on that thing all day long and not break it. This will be that Eagles kind of ballad.

Mark Miller: This was a good album. Really well built *as an album*. There were the hits, then there were great album tracks like "Victim of the Game."

Trisha Yearwood: I would get the call, and I would get nervous and excited about coming in and singing. Always casual, always Garth, Allen, and Mark. Allen would always make it easy. We'd start by listening to what they had so far, then we would talk about what we thought could be added. Then I would go in and sing.

Allen gave you a level of total comfort so that you were confident to try anything. Garth learned that from Allen and was the same way. "It's just tape," was what he said very often. I think, like any really good producer, Allen treated background vocals like the other instruments. He let you do your thing, and if you needed direction, he would give it to you. But Allen always thought it would come from a better place if each instrument found their part on their own.

G: Mark Sanders, one of the most decorated writers in this town. I've only written with him twice, and both times he brought songs I just adored, and I don't know why we didn't write three times. When we sat down, I said, "Here's an idea I got," and it hinged on

that title line. But probably the coolest thing about that song was how it played on piano. It was all written on guitar, but I loved how it moved over to where piano was the lead instrument, over to Bobby Wood. Again, big harmonies, but unlike Haggard's three stacked harmonies, this was more like the Eagles. Really, you've got a rock song, a big power ballad, but look what that steel does, it frames it right back into country music.

But here's where I'm beginning to show where I come from, and that's a time when FM radio was king, and groups like Queen, the Eagles, Zeppelin, rock groups were the thing you heard. And there were some great musical parts of that experience. I wasn't in an exclusive relationship with one genre. And by the time of *No Fences,* I'm beginning to draw more freely on what I found back there. I was an American kid, raised on a bunch of different streams of music. Some of the good things I found there could, I just knew, transfer over.

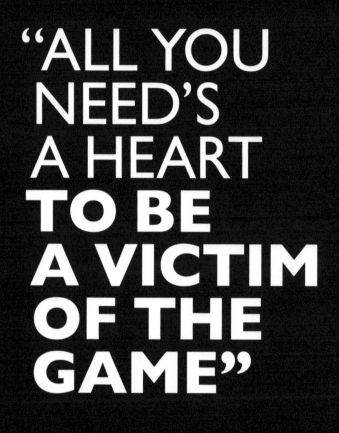

"ALL YOU NEED'S A HEART **TO BE A VICTIM OF THE GAME**"

Top row, left to right: Rob Hajacos (Fiddle), Milton Sledge (Drums), Mark Casstevens (Acoustic Guitar), Bobby Wood (Keyboards), and Chris Leuzinger (Electric Guitar).
Bottom row, left to right: Mark Miller (Engineer), Mike Chapman (Bass) Bruce Bouton (Steel), Garth, and Allen Reynolds (Producer).

THIS NEEDS TO BE LIKE A BAR BAND, **LIKE A BUNCH OF GUYS PLAYING THE END OF THE NIGHT,** LAST SONG OF THE SET KIND OF THING.
- CHRIS LEUZINGER

FRIENDS IN LOW PLACES

BY DEWAYNE BLACKWELL AND EARL "BUD" LEE

G: Going from "The Dance" into "Friends in Low Places," as singles, that's the one-two punch that put us in our own light, on our own plane. Not above anybody or different, but that's the one that, at that point, made us. There were a group of artists they called "hat acts" at the time. You're in there because you wore a hat, but then we came with "The Dance," something else altogether, *then* into "Friends in Low Places" and, *No, this guy is a country artist!* That back to back, I can tell you, we still haven't caught up from that combination yet.

Bob Doyle: Garth sang on the demo of "Friends in Low Places" around the time we signed the record deal and had that in his head. We got out on the road and, if you looked at the first album, there was not a lot that was really up-tempo, and so he was trying to add songs and find songs that would give him a little more for his show. He did a number of cover songs, "Keep Your Hands to Yourself," a Billy Joel thing, just to build the energy. Then he started doing "Friends in Low Places." It worked

1990 | Left to right: DeWayne Blackwell, Garth, and Earl "Bud" Lee at the #1 party for "Friends in Low Places."

very, very well. But we discovered that "Friends" had been recorded by someone else, and Garth was a little concerned and went to the writer, DeWayne Blackwell, and he said, "Geez, DeWayne, I thought you guys were going to hold that for me."

G: When we hit the road in mid-1989, the first album has been out two months, and we're doing "Friends in Low Places" at every show, right, before we ever record it. So, when they called and said the song's open—George Strait had passed on it—I asked, "Can I put it on hold?" They said, "You bet." So I put it on hold. But we had it on hold for a year, and DeWayne Blackwell, the writer, gets nervous because we've got it on hold for that long, and so he pitches it to another artist, named Mark Chesnutt. Chesnutt cuts it, and it's going to be his first single. Now, we've been playing this thing for a year and a half. We know the power, and, man, it gets tense. So I go to Blackwell, and say, "Hey, man, here's the deal, if Chesnutt's going to cut it, I can't put it on my record.

first single, then we can have it on both records." Because their version was coming out later, and if we did it as the first single, that would be quite a bit before. He said, "Would you guys guarantee first single?" And I said, "Hell yes."

Chris Leuzinger: They told the band, "This needs to be like a bar band, like a bunch of guys playing the end of the night, last song of the set kind of thing." Usually we were all trained to be very polite in our playing, meaning like I would never think about covering up a steel lick with a guitar lick or covering up a fiddle lick. But Garth was like, "No, you guys, I just want you to play like you're in a band. So it sounds like a band jamming onstage."

Allen Reynolds: It's got the humor and it's got the sing-along. We had fifty-some-odd people in here singing on that. Garth was orchestrating it from out in the studio, and so, you know, it was probably like clubs he played in Oklahoma. As long as that record's been out, people still say, "I thought I heard somebody opening a can of beer on that." Yeah, you did.

Mark Miller: Jimmy Bowen, who was running the label over at Capitol, had asked Allen to get as much of that guy he saw live as Allen could in the studio. I think "Friends in Low Places" is where we kind of first achieved that, got that energy to happen in a big way.

G: It was wild, but I'm telling you. I'm driving at about two o'clock in the morning back up from the studio. I'm driving and this DJ comes on and says, "In my entire career, I've never

ADAM LOOKS AT EVE AND SAYS, "STAND BACK, **I DON'T KNOW HOW BIG THIS THING GETS."** - g

So, it's going to be your call." They came back and said, "Well, Chesnutt's people said if you guarantee it's your

had so many requests for one song, this has to be the most requested song I've ever known." And then it comes, Mark Casstevens's guitar part.

1990 | The background singers for "Friends in Low Places" sit out front on the steps of Jack's Tracks.

I'm yelling, I've got my hands up in the air! We are on a ride that … we have no idea. You know there's that great Adam and Eve joke, when Adam looks at Eve and says, "Stand back, I don't know how big this thing gets." We don't have a real sense for what's getting ready to happen, none of us do. We would roll into clubs during this time, and every club owner would go, "You guys don't have a clue how big you are, do you?" But we were just guys from Oklahoma and Kansas, man, having fun. We didn't care. We just wanted to play. Wanted to play for girls. We wanted our *food* free. But this record starts to happen. They ordered a banner for Music Row, announcing "NO FENCES has gone platinum!" By the time it came back from the printer, they had to hand paint an "s" on "platinum(s)."

WILD HORSES

BY BILL SHORE AND DAVID WILLS

Allen Reynolds: That was another one with the Western motif, and Garth just loved that song. The rodeo thing was important to him, he wanted it represented on every album.

G: Yeah, saluting those men and women with hats. Every record will have at least one. It's a theme that anybody can get into. Bill Shore and David Wills. This was just one of these things that came like "Alabama Clay." We've played it live a thousand times, and it just keeps working. I've always loved it when a song takes you to a really specific place. "From a

I'VE ALWAYS LOVED IT WHEN **A SONG TAKES YOU TO A REALLY SPECIFIC PLACE.** - g

phone booth in Cheyenne." Boom, that's where you're at. "I made a promise to Diane." It's real specific but, at the same time, shit, we've all been there.

Allen Reynolds: I told him there was a girl he sang with, Trisha Yearwood. I just loved the buzz their two voices made together.

Trisha Yearwood: Allen loved what he called the "buzz" between our voices. "Wild Horses" was challenging for me. This was George Strait for Garth, new for me. This was also a harmony Garth could have sung himself. He and I can sound so much alike that sometimes I can't tell if it's him or me singing certain lines. I think that is a true sign of how well our voices blend.

G: We did harmony with each other really well. Did the same kind of licks, all this stuff. It was almost like we were raised the same on

(Top) 1992 | Garth and journalist Melinda Newman meet for the first time.

(Bottom) Garth with parents, Colleen and Raymond.

the same music. So Allen says, "Bring her in, let's see what happens." And her vocal quality on "Wild Horses"—she's got this vocal range that she can sing Broadway, she can do anything, but she can also sound like a cowgirl without trying if you put her in a rodeo song. We had her on "Wild Horses," "Victim of the Game," "New Way to Fly," she'd be all over these records from here on out. You'll be hearing the Trisha Yearwood influence on the music. As much as the players that played it, she was the Garth Brooks sound.

UNANSWERED PRAYERS

Words and Music by
LARRY B. BASTIAN, PAT ALGER
and GARTH BROOKS

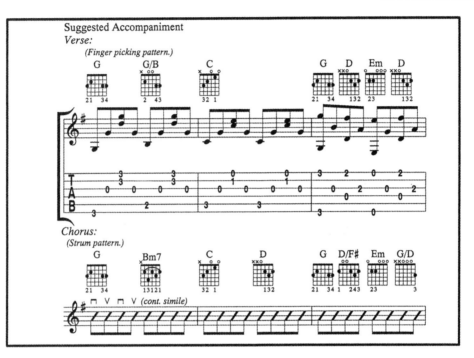

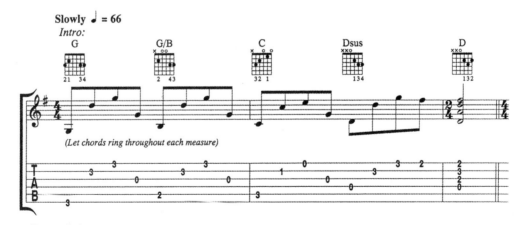

(Let chords ring throughout each measure)

Unanswered Prayers – 6 – 1
P0942EGX

UNANSWERED PRAYERS

BY PAT ALGER, LARRY BASTIAN AND GARTH BROOKS

Mark Miller: People just fell in love with this one when they heard it because everyone could see themselves going to their high school reunion. Thank God for unanswered prayers because, you know, we all have that fantasy of … what if I'd stayed with her?

G: Pat Alger and I sit down to write this story of meeting your high school sweetheart. This particular high school sweetheart I had in mind, it was weird, I had never, ever given so much to a relationship to get nothing back. This was one of the things where it was just a puppy on a string thing, and, you know, if you saw it happen to one of your other buddies you'd think, *I would never let that happen to me.* But when you're right in the middle of it, you can't help it. She was a doll. Gorgeous, sang, did all that stuff. Never gave me the time of day. Then I saw her a few years later; I was married. She was still gorgeous. Fantastic. But it worked better for the song for her not to be quite that, you know? But I like how a fragment, some moment in life, can become a full-blown story. The details may change, but you get the thought across, and what a story it became.

Pat Alger: As a songwriter, I'm looking for that place where I can get inside that story. So when Garth started talking about this idea, I was reflecting on something that had happened to me when I was in high school, just homing in on what Garth was saying. I wasn't really thinking very much about the universality of the idea at the moment we were doing it. I was just thinking of … this is a difficult story to tell in

1991 | Garth and Pat Alger.

I HAD NEVER, EVER GIVEN SO MUCH TO A RELATIONSHIP **TO GET NOTHING BACK.** - g verses and a chorus. But I knew people would connect with that idea of, well, she wasn't quite the angel I remember in my dreams.

Bob Doyle: "Unanswered Prayers" was an idea that Garth had had and couldn't quite get his head around as far as how to make it pay off. He was talking to Larry Bastian, and he described the scenario of the song.

G: I mean, me and Pat Alger have this song. We've got everything but the freaking hook. Everything. We've got the story, it's all working. So I'm writing with Larry Bastian, and we go walking here in Nashville and I go, "Hey, Larry, while we're walking, I have this song…" He goes, "Tell me a little about it." So I tell him the whole story and he goes, "Oh that's easy." I go, "Oh, really?" And he goes, "Yeah, it's unanswered prayers." First of all, I'm thinking "unanswered prayers" ain't going to sing that well. But I want to understand what he's getting at, so, okay, I ask him, "Why unanswered prayers?" He goes, "You're going to find out, some of God's greatest gifts ever are unanswered prayers."

Larry Bastian: Bob Doyle said he saw Garth one time in a show in Vegas where Garth said he still had the scars on his shins from stumbling up the stairs to write that line down. *(laughs)* But I didn't say it to Garth because I wanted part of the song. He just asked me a question, and I gave him an answer. I didn't even know that I was on the song as a writer until the song came out. Not that I'm giving the money back! But that says a lot about Garth Brooks, too, because he could have taken that and said, "Well, Larry gave me this." Because I had.

Pat Alger: Whatever went on between Larry and Garth, only they know. I wasn't there. In fact, Garth forgot to tell me about that until the person that did the administration from our publishing company, she said, "Who's Larry Bastian?" I said, "I don't know. Who *is* Larry Bastian?" She said, "Well he's a writer on your

song." I went, "Well, that is funny." But as I found out, we couldn't have done it without him, that's for sure. Garth just decided he's going to do what he's going to do and give him part of his share. At that point, I hadn't met Larry. But Garth always knows what the right thing to do is, and he does it.

G: The fact that I had the story wasn't much, made me the least of the three writers, isn't that crazy? Because when you think you have the story, okay. Pat Alger took that story and turned it into a poem, a great little saga, kind of like a little epic, a little movie, but then it was Larry Bastian that turned it into a song. It became an anthem, a thing that people hung up on their walls to get over shit or make peace with the idea that, Hey, this door closed, but there must be another door opening somewhere. When Pat and I first played it at The Bluebird, just trying it out with an audience, it was the only time in my career, or life, playing a song for the first time for an audience and after the first chorus, they stand up and applaud while you're still playing it. Me and Pat just looked at each other.

UN-ANSWERED PRAYERS

D♭

Acc. Gait

INTRO: 1 1₃ 4 5 5ˢ 5̄ᵀ

ᴬᴸᵀ

V. 1 1₃ 4 4   1 5₇ 6-1₅ 2-5

4 3- 6-5 4 1₃ 2- 1₃ 4 5ˢ 5̄ᵀ

V. ᴵᴺ ◇ 1 1₃ 4 4 1 5₇ 6-1₅ 2-5

4 3- 6-5 4 1₃ 2- 1₃ 5ˢ 5ˢ 5̄ᵀ

Cho: 1ⁿ₁₃ 4 5 1 5₇ 6-1₅ 2-5

1 1ⁿ 4 2̄ᵀ ⌐ 1 6-2-5   1 1₃ 4 5ˢ 5̄ᵀ
Loʳ

V: 1 1₃ 4 4 1 5₇ 6-1₅ 2-5

4 3- 6-5 4 1₃ 2- 1₃ 5ˢ 5ˢ 5 5

Brdg: 4̄ᵀ ⌐3̄ᵀ- `6- 2- 1₃ 4 5ˢ 5ˢ 5̄ᵀ 5⌐6⌐7
                                          ₂₃ QTR ◇ 567

1̄ᵀ 1₂₃ 4 5 1 5₇ 6-1₅ 2-5

1 1ⁿ 4 2̄ᵀ ⌐ 1 6-2-5 1 6-2-5
         Mid   Hi

1 6-2-5 1 1₃ 4 15 1̄ᵀ
 ᴴⁱ   5

SAME OLD STORY

BY TONY ARATA

Tony Arata: I'd made an album, and trust me, nobody knew about it, including MCA Records, the company that put it out. But there was a song on there that I wrote when Jamie, my wife, and I were living in Savannah called "Same Old Story." So one of the first things Garth did when we struck up a friendship was he started singing that song to me.

G: Tony Arata was the writer behind "The Dance." You know, you loved his writing so much that at some point you're hoping there's more you're going to do of Tony's. The melody on this thing killed me, and what I love is for a song's statement to have room for everybody. That's what I love about the Bible, a thousand people can read it and you're going to get a thousand different opinions of what they just read. In a song, when you start it, and in that first verse you hear about one situation, and in the second verse it's talking about another situation, how beautiful is that, that build? Tony's the master of that. And everybody finds a little of themselves in there.

BUT THERE'S SOMETHING ABOUT BEING IN THAT PAIN *IN A SONG.* **I LOVE THAT FEELING.** - g

Tony Arata: Garth said something like, "I just love the song, and I want to do it." It wasn't, "I hear this as a single for the radio," so much as, "I hear it as a part of this album." And I honestly don't know how many others

Tony Arata and Garth.

there are like that. So, yeah, that was one of the greatest fortunes of all, was to run across somebody who believed in the album format, who wasn't just saying, "Okay, we need four singles and then five of some other stuff to fill it out." Every album meant something. All the songs meant something and had a particular spot on the record. Both he and Allen thought like that.

G: When Hollywood does films about songwriters, especially country songwriters, when they are going through the shit is when they write their best songs. They always do that. It's always, "Sorry we broke up, but here comes four number one hits right here." But there's something about being in that pain *in a song.* I love that feeling. "Same Old Story," man, it takes you there.

MR. BLUE

BY DEWAYNE BLACKWELL

G: When DeWayne said he wrote it, I went, "Shit, I love that song." He says, "You don't even know that song." So I sang it to him. I said, "Remember, I'm the last of six kids, that song was blaring in our house all the time, we grew up with that kind of stuff." It was his first single as a writer, in 1959. Now it's on *No Fences*, the same record as another of his songs, "Friends in Low Places." But man, DeWayne Blackwell, this is the very same man who wrote "I'm Gonna Hire a Wino to Decorate Our Home" for David Frizzell. That man was packing some history.

Bob Doyle: I think as a band in dance halls in Oklahoma, you had to play a little bit of everything, and credibly, otherwise you didn't keep working. "Mr. Blue" comes from a deep well Garth draws on.

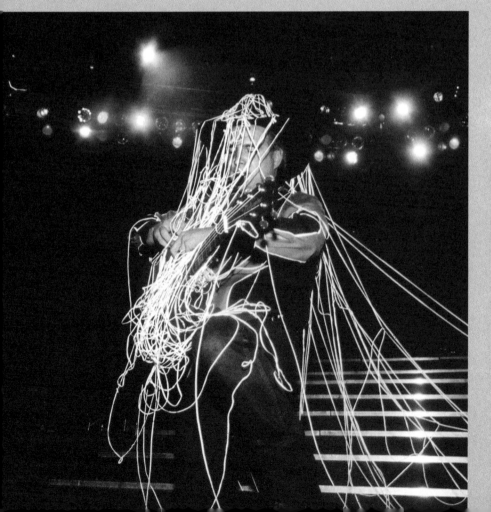

THE WAY NASHVILLE SESSIONS ARE DONE, **A LOT OF FREEDOM IS GIVEN TO THE PLAYERS,** AND THEY DELIVER AMAZINGLY.
- ALLEN REYNOLDS

Mark Miller: I remember this song from when I was a kid. It's kind of like late fifties. But Garth put a real kind of country swing to it and it worked great.

G: In Oklahoma you can swing the hell out of a song. The dance floor wanted it, so we'd bring it. That Western swing part of country music is so right for me. I wanted a swing tune on every record, and this was the one for *No Fences*.

Allen Reynolds: There's a lot here that's just Rob and his style of fiddle playing. The things that happen on a session are most often the result of just the whole group making suggestions to one another and that interchange, that dynamic. Some things happen because Garth is asking for a certain musician to do something, not always real specific, filling something in someplace, but the final result is very much out of the musicians' heads. The way Nashville sessions are done, a lot of freedom is given to the players, and they deliver amazingly. I'd always come to the studio with a fallback thing in my mind but do my best to stay off talkback and encourage the flow of ideas, just to see what they'd conjure, because they're so good.

G: A lot of that old Haggard stuff was kind of a salute to Bob Wills. If you go to any of the cowboy bands, the real authentic ones, they had a clarinet player and a saxophone player, and sometimes it was the same guy playing both of them at the same time out of both sides of his mouth. It's all that big band meets cowboy stuff, really fun to do. And to play that for DeWayne Blackwell, and for him to go, "I feel like I'm a teenager again," just like when he wrote it, that was sweet, to see a grown man cry because he got to hear that song again and to go someplace because of the music.

WOLVES

BY STEPHANIE DAVIS

Stephanie Davis: The farm crisis of the late eighties was in full swing back home in Montana. I mean, it seemed every call home brought more stories of bankruptcies and farm auctions. It always called to mind my grandparents' beautiful old homestead near Fishtail, Montana. After decades of working the place, nine kids, and a lot of hardship, they finally sold it in the late forties for next to nothing. As a kid, I'd see it out the window as we'd drive past and fantasize about making enough money to someday buy it back.

I must have had this on my mind the night I wrote it. I'd been typing term papers for college kids, a dollar a page. I was taking a break, just grabbed a guitar and wrote these couple verses. And very quickly my brain tells me, *Well, nobody on Music Row is going to cut this.* I'd had no luck for quite a while taking my songs around, and they were just not what—they were looking for three-minute, positive, up-tempo songs. So I wrote these verses and thought, *Well, it's kind of a dirge about people losing their ranch and stuff,* so I tossed it in the garbage. My boyfriend came back from his gig about 2:00 a.m., I think, and saw this thing lying in the garbage. Picks it out, says, "This is good."

G: I heard this song in '88. Me and Randy Taylor, the guy who wrote "Much Too Young," he was in town from Oklahoma. We were throw

THAT SONG RIPPED MY HEART OUT, PROBABLY BECAUSE IT WAS EXACTLY WHAT I WAS FEELING AT THAT TIME. - g

ing darts down at Douglas Corner. This little girl from Montana is up there singing, her and her guitar. And she goes, "This next song is on hold for Willie Nelson." Randy Taylor is a huge Willie Nelson fan. We look at each other and go, "Yeah, right." She starts to sing it. I don't know what happens over the next three minutes, but what I do know is that when it's over, I'm embarrassed, because I'm standing just feet away from her, standing there in front of everybody, just looking at her.

That song ripped my heart out, probably because it was exactly what I was feeling at that time. I just didn't want to be one of the failures.

Stephanie Davis: I think I did three songs at this writers' night. Now, I'd met Garth several months before, but this time he was dressed differently. He had these terrible Bermuda shorts on and his ball cap on backwards, playing darts in the back. I just didn't recognize him. When I got to "Wolves," not many other people are listening, but this guy just started slowly walking up to the stage until he's standing there in front of me, holding this dart in his hand, kind of pointing it at me.

Bob Doyle: She was just one of those great storytellers, and "Wolves," to me, said so much about what was happening at that point in our world, too, with farmers and people losing their farms and people losing them as a result of foreclosures and the banks. It was, I think, a real honest song.

G: In Oklahoma, there were the two kinds of people: poor with land and poor without. But these guys that had it, they're fighting like hell just to hang on to it. That story hit me like a ton of bricks.

I talked to her afterwards, and said, "If Willie doesn't do that, I have a deal and we're working on the record right now."

Stephanie Davis: I didn't even say anything, I was just so stunned. Nobody had ever said much positive about that song. Then he turned around and went back to his dart game. I remember that night also because somebody had broken into my car and stolen my radio.

Willie did not record the song, and it was only a short time later, maybe a month or two, the phone rang well after midnight, and it was Garth. He said, "Hey, I'm in the studio and we just cut "Wolves," would you like to hear it?"

He played it over the phone. And, you know, I just sat on the living room floor of my little place and cried like a baby because, not just because somebody had cut my song, but because his record of it was so true, so perfect. I heard this song through another's ears for the first time, and I know it sounds kind of corny, but I thought it had strength and majesty, and it was kind of a powerful lesson to me about shutting out others' opinions and just writing your stuff and telling your stories. You know, it's very difficult if you're here in Nashville and you have $100 to your name, it's very difficult to be that strong and believe in yourself.

I got what for me were some big, fat royalty checks, and I had my dad go out looking for a little piece of land out there in Montana, something near where my grandparents had a farm. I did buy one, not too far away from there, and it was the realization of a dream.

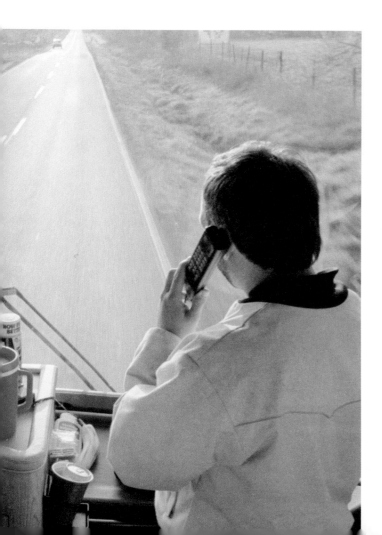

I CRIED LIKE A BABY … BECAUSE HIS RECORD OF IT WAS **SO TRUE, SO PERFECT.**
- STEPHANIE DAVIS

A GREAT PRODUCER KNOWS GREAT SONGS

1991 | Garth and Allen Reynolds.

LOVED MY DAD, and nobody on this planet is going to be my dad but my dad, but if I would ever have a second father, ever, it would be Allen Reynolds. My father was a Korean War veteran, U.S. Marine Corps, a Golden Gloves boxing champ, and I'm telling you, even at seventy years old you still respectably feared the man, like if he got mad enough he could take care of business. But there was safety there, and the day a man like that passes away it's like taking the top off the car and there is nothing between you and the stars anymore. There's not that protective coat. Same thing with Allen Reynolds. There was a protection there. There was that protection, and, thank God, in this house, this studio, I always felt it. This place is an oasis in the desert, man. Especially as the business got more complicated. Allen made it a safe place, where music could be made without the world outside knocking every ten minutes.

Allen came to Nashville from Arkansas, via Memphis. He taught English at Elvis Presley's high school, Humes High, and worked in a bank. One of his closest pals was Dickey Lee, who wrote "She Thinks I Still Care." He and Dickey work for Jack Clement after Jack leaves Sam Phillips's Sun Studio. I mean, these guys were in the thick of it. Somewhere in there a song Allen writes, "Five O'Clock World," is a top five hit for The Vogues. You get the idea. By the time I meet Allen, he's seen this world of songs and records from just about every angle, and he knows how to get the job done. He's had hits with Kathy Mattea, Crystal Gayle, Hal Ketchum.

A lot of what Allen was after was about the great performance of a great song, so you had to start with the material. And, man, he knows songs. But once we had one, Allen didn't come in the studio telling the players what to do with it. He assembled the finest bunch of musicians you could get your hands on, and then he watched to see what would happen when he let them at that song. He gave those players the space to find their own way, to leave their mark on a record. He gave everyone that respect and that space, and damn if you don't hear it in the records. We didn't work with a click track, and we rarely worked from demos. Mostly I'd play the song on guitar, and in that world Allen created for songs, we'd see what happened. It wasn't always perfect, but Allen wasn't after perfect, he was after the realness of it. And he had a confidence about how he went after that. His confidence was strong enough for everybody in that room to share in it. You felt confident, and you felt safe trying whatever you needed to try. Like Allen would say, it was only tape.

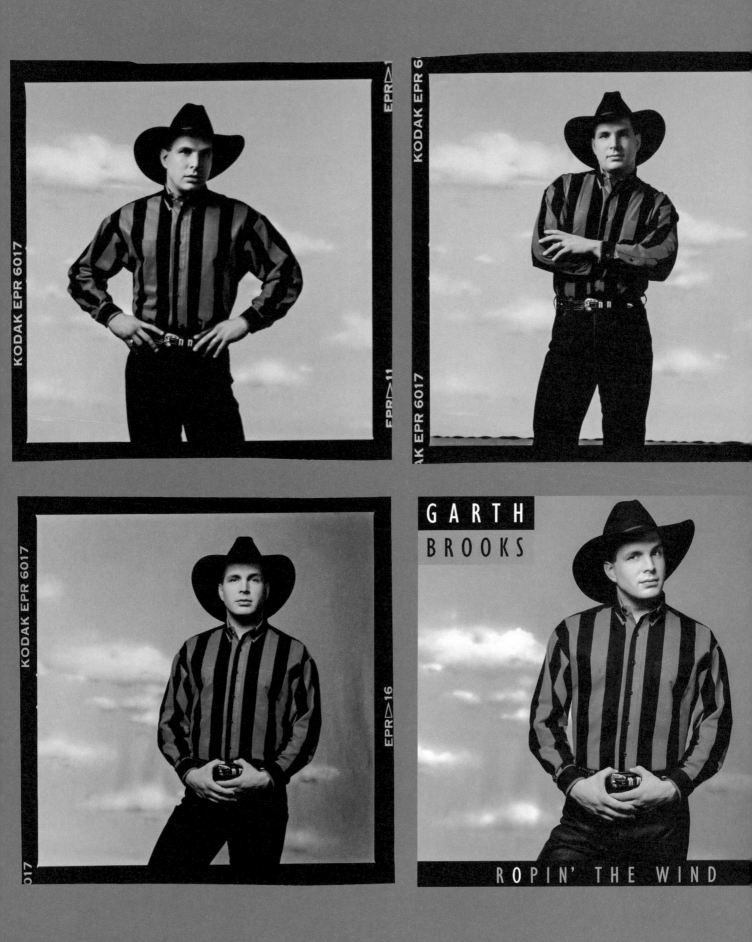

YEAR THREE

1991

Bev Parker always saw this album cover in front of endless blue skies. Pretty simple, really: cowboy hat, blue skies, a hint of a smile. It would be Jerry Joyner, a graphic design artist, who would make one letter white, that "O," there beside the rest, starting a long tradition of hidden messages in all things "Garth." *Ropin'* brought with it a full-color presentation. By contrast, the first two albums were very much like the black-and-white opening of *The Wizard of Oz,* with *Ropin'* being the full-color experience when we all get to take the journey down the yellow brick road. At the time, our career really was in full color, and the journey was taking all of us to places we had never been before.

1991 | TY ENGLAND AND I were college roommates at Oklahoma State. I'm a senior, he's a sophomore. So Ty is trying to live like I do. We're roommates in a dorm. I don't have to go to class in the morning. Being a senior, I got it down, I know exactly what my schedule is …only afternoon classes. Ty, you see, has to take all the 7:00 a.m. classes, because that's what they do with underclassmen. This guy is staying up with me until two or three in the morning, working on music, and then trying to get up and go to school. He lasts a while up there before his dad yanks his ass back home to Oklahoma City. And rightly so. But in that same year, that's when we made a pact with each other that, hey, if one of us gets there, if one of us gets a hold of the dream, he calls the other one. That was our pact. So I sign the record deal. I call Ty.

Ty is back there in Oklahoma, working a good job at a Sherwin-Williams paint store. Now, Ty's dad had a buddy that worked along with him at some point, and I don't know if your dad was like this, but the hand of God could come out of the sky and write something down and my dad would go, I'm not so sure about that, Bud…but if one of the guys at the *office* said it, *(laughing)* it was solid, right? It was that way growing up, like everybody's dad is that way.

So this guy that had worked with Ty's father had tried the music business before. I think he may have even tried to go to Nashville, and he told Mr. England, "Pal, your son would have better luck ropin' the wind than making a living in music."

A couple years later, we're playing Cowboys, one of the biggest honky-tonks in Dallas, and *No Fences* is just out, "Friends in Low Places" is just out, and this place is a zoo. It's exactly the way you want it. Off to the right and left of the stage, they would put tables for VIPs, and, well, the table on the right had Ty's parents sitting there, and I'm standing on that stage, looking at them during the show, and they're so proud of their boy. And I'm looking at that boy, and he's having such a great time playing music. And I go, *Hmm, maybe we're all out here just ropin' the wind.* That was the saying that stuck with me, and one day, I just went, *Oh my God, there it is.* Whatever the next record becomes, it's already got a title.

So, *Ropin' the Wind* was built in the middle of all hell breaking loose. And, yeah, I was scared. But what I forgot was Allen Reynolds is steering the ship, I'm not, and Allen didn't have any concerns about *Ropin' the Wind*, none at all. And so, this was … this was an album that just did the impossible. It followed one of the biggest-selling records in country music history. It was against all odds, and Allen Reynolds welcomed it.

Murfreesboro, TN, 1991 | Garth and Ty England playing together at MTSU.

AGAINST THE GRAIN

BY BRUCE BOUTON, LARRY CORDLE
AND CARL JACKSON

Early 80s | Mark Tate, Ty England, Paul Compton, Garth, and Dale Pierce.

IT WAS PROBABLY **THE MOST IN YOUR FACE** THING THAT WE HAD DONE YET. - g

Allen Reynolds: I remember him saying, "I could never get a big head, my family would beat my ass." As I got to know them, he's right, they would have.

G: That's Larry Cordle and Carl Jackson. It's also Bruce Bouton, who's playing all the steel on the records. "Against the Grain" kind of said everything about where we were at the time. We couldn't get too big for our britches because of all the success, that way of thinking just doesn't work. But, at the same time, we needed to stand by it and, you know, have a confidence about it all, a belief. And we believed we were country music, even if we also believed we were coming at it from a different angle. It was a good way to start *Ropin'*. That first song, like "The Thunder Rolls" on the last album, probably takes a risk at pissing people off, but we did that very first blast on this song, even delayed it a little bit after it hits, so maybe you

might turn your radio or whatever up, like, *Is this thing on?* Then, when it comes full on, it knocks you back. The response could go either way, but it kind of just said, *Look here*, was just a smack in the face and here we go, and it started the journey on *Ropin'*. It was probably the most in-your-face thing that we had done yet. This is how you start the record, and I can't imagine that song fitting anywhere else on it.

Bob Doyle: I just think Garth and Allen did a brilliant job of pulling together and sequencing and selecting songs that helped him continue to grow as an artist and bring his audience along, not in a radical way, or with too much of a shift, more like, *We did that and now we're going to do this.*

G: The first instrument I ever played was the banjo. Bluegrass was my thing. We'd go to the flat-picking championships way out in the parking lots. Bluegrass was everything for us and what we started with, all that sibling harmony, those soaring high harmonies of things like the Seldom Scene, New Grass Revival.

Harmony gives life, and harmony gives different angles to look at things, because the notes that they're singing are different notes. You'll look at a verse straight on, in one dimension or two dimensions, but when those harmonies hit in the chorus, it gets three-dimensional.

RODEO

BY LARRY BASTIAN

Larry Bastian: He'll take the song and he'll go in a direction that you wouldn't dream that anybody could take one of your songs. I'm talking about "Rodeo" now. He took that song and rocked the hell out of it.

G: I went all over this town trying to get "Rodeo" cut. Originally, the song was called "Miss Rodeo," and it was written for a woman to sing, and no one would sing it.

Larry Bastian: Yeah, it was a girl's song. It was called "Miss Rodeo," but Garth loved it. In fact, I played it for him when he was out here that first time. This was a song I had written probably six years or seven years before I met Garth, and it had been a, not a hit, but it had been recorded in Canada, Alberta, Canada, and it was on the Stampede, I think, a rodeo up there, but girls sang it. It was about a gal lamenting the fact that her guy was in love with the rodeo rather than her. Finally, Garth said to me, "I'm going to record it." I said, "You can't record it, it's a girl's song." He said, "Just watch me."

G: The original demo was this California country feel, and, yeah, it was a girl singing, but through it all you could hear the muscle, you could hear the sport of rodeo trying to come out of the song.

Chris Leuzinger: Bobby Wood moved to the electric piano and started playing that thing, and Milton just came up with that funky beat, and Mike, he just came in. . . I didn't have to do much but jump on board. No conversation. It just went that way.

Allen Reynolds: Garth and I just talked about what happened with that song. Because "Rodeo" didn't turn out like what he had in mind, either. But, yeah, I'd be a fool to deny the offerings that are there in the studio just because I was after my own vision. These guys bring so much creativity and experience to a song that I'd be crazy to get in the way, I'd be cheating everybody if I didn't allow that. And "Rodeo," that song kind of led us all, took us where it wanted to go. Songs can do that.

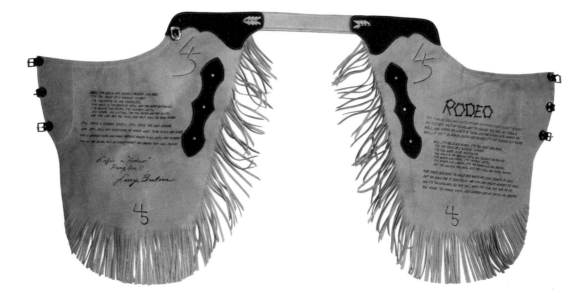

Larry Bastian gifted Bob Doyle these chaps with the words to the number-one song branded into the leather and signed with the famous quote "Life's a Rodeo, Hang On!"

G: Bobby's electric piano was a result of the slimy, greasy shit that Milton Sledge was laying down on his drum kit. Milton has a wonderful cadence. It's dripping with sweat, and Bobby, who is constantly on the backside of everything, just slid right in there. And when that happened, you saw Chapman's ears perk up, the Muscle Shoals bass player, and all the sudden this thing got nasty. It got really good, really quick.

Larry Bastian: He played it for me at the studio. He wanted me to hear it, and he, I think he didn't know what I'd say about it because it was so different from what I'd written. He changed the lyric around to fit him, but it'd been kind of a lament, the way it was written, and now it was a rocker. I'd have never thought of that. The young gals and guys in their teens just absolutely went nuts over it, and they still play it. I still hear that one.

G: We were thinking about singles, and I said to Jimmy Bowen, "We got 'Shameless' on here, but I don't want to lead with it because I'm afraid we're going to scare people to death with it." I said, "I don't know what a first single could be." He says, "For me, obviously, it's 'Rodeo.'" I never would have guessed. But what

a great, great choice that kind of defined *Ropin'*. It was still a cowboy tune like "Much Too Young," but it had a different set of clothes on it. When Chris LeDoux pulled me over and said, "Man, 'Rodeo' is what cowboy music is all about," those two votes of confidence for "Rodeo" really set it on its way. It's one of those songs that has surprised me in my career. That thing just doesn't go away.

I SAID, "YOU CAN'T RECORD IT, IT'S A GIRL'S SONG."

HE SAID, "JUST WATCH ME."
- LARRY BASTIAN

WHAT SHE'S DOING NOW

BY PAT ALGER AND GARTH BROOKS

HE DIDN'T SAY SHE'S
TENDING BAR OR SOMETHING
LIKE THAT, HE SAID,
**"WELL, SHE'S KEEPING
ME UP AT NIGHT."**
- PAT ALGER

Mark Miller: This studio's the place we've made all the records, but it's always been more, you know, a clubhouse sometimes, a place where people liked to hang, mostly musicians and songwriters. Early on Garth would come in and sing some of the demos for our songwriters who'd be writing here, including a guy named Pat Alger.

Pat Alger: I was a good bit older than most of these guys except for Larry Bastian, about ten years older, well, fourteen years older than Garth and, I think, ten years older than Tony and Kent. So I was having a different experience than these guys, probably. I'd spent the first ten years of my career playing live music all over the place, and it never occurred to me to pitch any of my songs until somebody cut one of them and I got some money in the mail. So, I never really got the bug to be whatever you call it, a journeyman songwriter, not until then. By the time Garth came along, I had some experience, I'd had some pretty good cuts by then, but only had about three hits, maybe. I was still trying to figure it out, to be honest with you. He just came around at the right time. But, I mean, no one ever expects something like that, you never expect anything like that to be the defining moment of your career. We were just writing songs. Always good ones with him, but still, just writing songs.

G: When you sit down with Pat, if you have a story of an old lover, he can pull it out of you and

he can put it to music in a way that makes it so believable. And I've been lucky enough in my life to meet and share time with some great women who all probably would've been just phenomenal partners in life, just the sweetest people. So that makes for a lot of great content to write about, because it's a joy to sing about these relationships. They were all very innocent in one way and very adventurous in another, you know, you're just finding out who you are and you learn so much from each one. You swear that if you saw them today you'd just hug them and cry, because it was just a sweet, sweet time in your life.

Allen Reynolds: That's another one that he and Pat wrote upstairs here. Another song they gave away, this time to Crystal Gayle. Garth had this idea about someone from his past, and he's wondering what she's doing now, but as they talked about it and were getting into the song, Pat heard that and said, "You don't know what you got, do you?" And he put this spin on it, or he *found* the spin that was sitting there kind of waiting for them. That was the spark, I think.

Pat Alger: That was a real interesting day. He came in

and he said, "I have a past girlfriend that lives out in Colorado and I want to write a song about her." I also happened to have an ex-girlfriend in Colorado, so that made it a little easier.

So I said to him, "What about her?" He said, "You know, just what she's doing now." And I went, "Well, what's she doing now?" And that's the way we did a lot of it, we just talked it out. But when I asked him that, he didn't say she's tending bar or something like that, he said, "Well, she's keeping me up at night."

G: I remember him looking up at me, because I was always pacing, he was always sitting. But I remember him looking up at me with his glasses, he goes, "I wonder if *she* knows what she's doing now." At the time, you know, all you're trying to do is get this message across to someone in your past, hoping that she'll hear it some day and go, "Okay, cool, he enjoyed the time we spent together." But Pat had turned the idea of "what is she doing now?" on its head. He turned the whole song on its head, really, made it a song.

Pat Alger: After that, we wrote it in about twenty minutes. It was really easy

THE DEEPNESS OF THAT FEELING OF HOW SOMETHING UNFINISHED CAN STILL JUST KEEP YOU UP AT NIGHT YEARS LATER.
- PAT ALGER

because we knew what we were writing about. What we were really talking about was the feeling, the deepness of that feeling of how something unfinished can still just keep you up at night years later.

G: I thought that was a beautiful, beautiful sentiment, and, again, the music, its color, kind of matched the sentiment. "I took a walk in the winter wind." That whole line right there feels kind of light blue, kind of icy blue, and the music captured that.

"I CAN HEAR HER CALL EACH TIME THE COLD WIND BLOWS AND I WONDER IF SHE KNOWS ... WHAT SHE'S DOIN' NOW"

BURNING BRIDGES

BY STEPHANIE C. BROWN AND GARTH BROOKS

Charlotte, NC, 1992 | Stephanie Brown and Garth.

G: Stephanie Brown, she was who I was introduced to when I moved to town, the night I got here. She's the woman that said, "I've got a friend named Bob Doyle that I want to introduce you to." So Stephanie was my way in to the music business. Then she became my landlady, and so we would write together. She was a writer and a publisher. But, I mean, she introduced me to Bob Doyle, of course Bob's the reason why I'm sitting here. And so, this is a good relationship. She's a little bit older than I am, and she's very, very wise. She's an English teacher, so she's very articulate.

Bob Doyle: You remember, Garth's landlady gave me a tape of "Much Too Young"? Only in Nashville, right? That was Stephanie Brown.

Stephanie Brown: I introduced him to Bob, because I told Garth that he needed two things: He needed somebody with influence and money, and I didn't have either one. I had some influence, but not enough, so I introduced him to Bob, and you know the rest of that story.

Bob Doyle: Well, I mortgaged my house, *then* I had some money. *(laughs)*

Stephanie Brown: I remember when Garth'd come and play me demos, at that point he and Sandy were living in the house. I had one apartment and they had the other. I remember him playing "If Tomorrow Never Comes," just a little cassette on the refrigerator, a player on top of his refrigerator, and he was proud, really of that song in particular. But we wrote some stuff, and "Burning Bridges" was one of them.

G: Songs do something in our lives that's unlike anything else. They have in mine, that's

for sure. I know there are so many things that I fear that Dan Fogelberg touched on so beautifully, so when I'd listen to his records I'd live in that fear with him, and it made me feel a little less scared because someone's in the boat with me. That's a wonderful, wonderful thing.

I like to think the music of "Burning Bridges" comforted those people that were not stick-arounders, the people that burned bridges even though they didn't mean to, because the only way they knew how to go about what they do was to leave. Some people are just good at leaving, and that's what the character in this song was doing. In that sense, it's not a simple song. You know, we don't often think

UNTIL THAT FRONT DOOR DIDN'T SQUEAK, **HE COULDN'T LEAVE WITHOUT WAKING HER UP.**

- g

about the leaver in sympathetic terms, but I mean sometimes the leaver is the victim because they just don't have any way to be able to settle down, to commit. And the life they get is colored by that in every way. In a lot of ways, in my view, the people being left are better off than the person that can't stay. Because at some point, the people being left are going to find the person they're supposed to be with, but that person that's leaving all the time . . . never will. And that, to me, makes the villain the victim.

Mike Palmer, the drummer, who's like a brother to me on the road, we're playing this every night, and he comes up to me and goes, "I always thought the first line of this song was a throwaway line. 'Yesterday she thanked me for oiling that front door, this morning when she wakes she won't be thankful anymore.'"

Mike saw it like oiling the door was a chore. For a while there he didn't get it that until that front door didn't squeak, he couldn't leave without waking her up. And when it hit him, the song changed again.

Trisha Yearwood: That line is one of my favorite Garth Brooks lyrics *ever!*

G: It's a great thing as a writer when a line has that kind of time-release effect. It's one thing, for years, and then, *whoa*, it very suddenly takes you someplace brand-new, with that little shift in meaning. Good songs have layers.

PAPA LOVED MAMA

BY KIM WILLIAMS AND GARTH BROOKS

The studio message board and general BS collection :)

G: Kim brought this to me. If you notice, Kim Williams will now take off, from "Papa Loved Mama" on, now he's a staple in a Garth Brooks album because he brings the joy. He's the loud uncle. He's the guy that . . . this is going to be a shitty family reunion until he shows up, and then all the kids smile. The dogs are barking. That's who and what Kim Williams was to us. We already had the tenth cut on *Ropin'*, we're in here recording something else, and it was like a question of whether he was going to get it whipped into shape in time or not. And he did, and we recorded it. And I loved it. It's not a long song, there's not a lot in it. It's a very dark story, but it's an interesting story, and when Garth is through singing it, the band takes this long ride as this record goes out. It's this great kickass outro, and Bruce Bouton

> # AND IT WAS LIKE A QUESTION OF WHETHER HE WAS GOING TO GET IT WHIPPED INTO SHAPE IN TIME OR NOT. **AND HE DID, AND WE RECORDED IT. AND I LOVED IT.**
> ## - ALLEN REYNOLDS

which was Patsy Cline's "Walkin' After Midnight," and Kim brought this in on the last day of sessions. We had an open session, and we wrote it out on one of Chris's cartage cases out there in the front room. We got it far enough to be able to come in and kind of get it down, get it where the band could put a track to it. When Casstevens and Sledge started doing that little chunk-a-chunk thing up front, that was a lot of fun right there.

Allen Reynolds: That title line comes from an old folk saying that, I believe, was Carl Sandburg, like something he quoted or something he'd collected. Anyway, what I remember most is that up in the front room we had these anvil cases from Chris's gear, all these guitars and amps, and Kim Williams is writing the song with Garth, and they got it well underway, but it's not finished. Kim is out there with pencil and paper, leaning over one of those cases working on the song, while is playing a lap steel instead of his regular steel, and when Bruce gets on lap steel, he is one of the funkiest guys ever.

G: There was a newspaper story that kind of inspired this. But we hadn't seen it, just heard about it. Probably a month or two after we'd recorded the song, Kim found the newspaper, and there was a black-and-white photo. It wasn't a trailer, just the semi tractor itself, but it was buried into this no-tell motel kind of place. I mean, it's buried, the roof's down and everything. Now I don't know if the trucker just fell asleep and hit the place or what. I don't think it was planned like a murder or anything. But it gave us ingredients for a song.

Kim Williams loved that newspaper picture, man. He carried it everywhere. We got the song done just in time that day and felt like, *Oh, this one's going to be too much fun to pass on to another record, it has to go on this one.*

SHAMELESS

BY BILLY JOEL

Allen Reynolds: That was an important single for Garth. He was a big fan of Billy Joel's, and I remember him talking to me about that song, asking me what I thought, did I think we could do that. I had no problems with it myself, and part of the reason why was that he was so passionate about it. Passion is a big part of Garth anyway. He's a passionate guy, and this song just captured it.

It surprised me a little bit, only because of his early comments to me about love being a four-letter word and how he almost choked on the idea of singing lines even close to "I love you, baby." But this song is so driven, so strong,

"I'm shameless when it comes to loving you." And, man, when this came out, the teller at the bank was talking to me about it.

Mark Miller: Well, obviously that second record was a biggie. Something's going on here. I mean, like nothing before in my world, anyway, and probably not the town's world. So people are thinking a lot about what comes next. And then, look at the songs, I mean, "Shameless." *Ropin'* had a power.

G: My buddy Mark Sanders talked me into this Columbia House ten CDs for a dollar thing. So I signed up because he needed people to

sign up. Well, the thing was, I thought what you did was you picked all these CDs and then you just had to buy four or five over the next year at full price, no big deal. But no, no, no, they're going to send you these others, and if you don't send them back, you've just bought them at full price.

Well, we're gone for two months, three months. I come back and my box is full of mail, with five or six CDs I've never purchased, right? One of those CDs was Billy Joel's *Storm Front*. I hadn't bought a Billy Joel CD in a while. I love Billy Joel, but my life's gotten busy. But, I gotta tell you, *Storm Front* might be one of the greatest, if not the greatest Billy Joel record ever. And there's a song on there called "Shameless" that's just sex on a record. I want to sing right there.

I watched him with that record, and the first single goes by, second single, third single, so I personally make the call to the record label, ask if they can put me in touch with Billy's management. His group says they're not thinking about putting it out as a single. I said,

"Would you give us your blessing?" They said, "Go for it."

Chris Leuzinger: Cutting that song was just a vibey thing. It just really hit me, and I'd have to say the *way* we cut it just kind of brought us into some new territory for Garth. He and Allen were always taking it one step forward.

G: Let's just look at it this way. Country music is blowing up everything at this point. Jimmy Bowen's Capitol Nashville is, I'm going to say, probably close to eighty percent of EMI's bottom line worldwide. They are selling that much product. So Bowen understands that he sees spikes when ballads come out. Record sales go up. So we went five singles deep on *Ropin'*, with the three ballads: "Shameless," "What She's Doing Now," and "The River." All of them very, very different from each other, all of them with their own unique sound. But "Shameless" was the scary one. Oh, man! We did the CMA show and debuted "Shameless" on it.

When it ends, when we're done playing, nothing. Nothing. I am, in my gut and soul, I am panicking. I'm thinking, *Oh shit, I have just, I just broke the ship. We just crashed.* Then, slowly, this wave of applause comes after this silence, and it keeps going, and that just sets you on your heels, and now you're thinking, *Holy crap. We might be onto something.* It was an odd three to four seconds for me at the CMAs, I had flown to the highest, crashed, and then flown back to the highest again. It was a roller coaster, I can tell you.

1991 | Backstage at the Country Music Awards.

Trisha Yearwood: I have a vivid memory of doing this song in the studio, because he brought me in to do the harmony and he really wanted me to wail on the end. He always complained, saying, "You just open your mouth and you'll hit this note that's amazing and you don't even look like it takes effort." That day, he said, "I at least want you to make it *look* hard." So I was hitting these notes and I was feeling really good about myself, because I'm wailing. But he's not getting what he wants. He wants it to be a lot more kind of passionate or more gritty, I guess, and so I'm singing but getting frustrated, which is a nice way to say it, because I'm like, "I am singing my ass off here," and he's saying, "No, let's try it again." Now I'm getting pissed off, and finally he says something like, "I know you can sing it, but I know you're not giving me one hundred percent, I know you can give me something more." I was like, "Alright here, roll the tape," and I was just angry and I just unleashed, and I hear him in the booth going, "There it is, there it is."

When I hear that song and hear myself at the end, I just remember how mad I was at him for pushing me. But, really, he was great about encouraging me, going, "Hey, the worst thing that can happen is you can totally go off some place you didn't mean to go and we erase it." He's like, "This is a safe place to make a mistake." I learned a lot about that with him. Made me a little braver, like, let it rip and let's see what happens.

G: When we put Trisha Yearwood's wailing vocals on top of it on the way out, I thought, *Oh crap, this is so, so good, but this is going to be a hard record for country radio,* just because it doesn't sound like anything else. But it ended up working, in part because of Bruce Bouton's steel playing. It was beautiful, and that's what brought this rock or pop record back into the country field.

New York, NY, 1992 | "Good Morning America."

SLOWLY, THIS WAVE OF APPLAUSE COMES AFTER THIS SILENCE, AND IT KEEPS GOING, AND THAT JUST SETS YOU ON YOUR HEELS. - g

COLD SHOULDER

BY KENT BLAZY, KIM WILLIAMS
AND GARTH BROOKS

Left to right: Garth, Allen Reynolds, and Mark Miller in the control room at Jack's Tracks.

Kent Blazy: Garth brought in a couple different people that he was writing with to try to see if we could all write some things together, and the biggest life changer for me was when he called me up one day and said, "Hey, I'm writing with this kid Kim Williams, and I played him one of the songs that we wrote and he hated it, but he liked one of the lines in there and thought that would be a good title for a song. Would you want to write with him?"

It's that same kind of thing that happened with "If Tomorrow Never Comes," when he said, "The twenty-five people that listened hated this idea, you want to work on it?" Well, I thought, *So this other guy hates my song, but you want me to write with him. Sure.*

G: Oh, yes indeed, Kent Blazy and Kim Williams. It's those writing sessions with these two guys that you just smiled all the way driving there. You knew it was going to be fun. You knew it was going to be no egos. You knew it was going to be brothers. Kent Blazy had enough energy to run everybody. Kim Williams? You tried to write as much as you could before he fell asleep on you. And you laughed. You laughed the whole time.

Kent Blazy: Garth and Kim and I got together, and the interesting thing was Garth had never told me that Kim Williams had been burned over ninety percent of his body. So the day comes and Kim showed up first, because he was always very much on time, and it was pretty much a shock. I had never probably seen anybody with burns and scars like that. Then, after like half an hour of being with him, I totally forgot about it. Never thought about it ever again, in fact.

G: I'd gone home for Christmas, and driving home I noticed there on Christmas Eve this semi-tractor trailer rig with the triangles out,

DAMN, DAMN. IF YOU'VE EVER BEEN A DRINKER, THAT'S MUSIC TO DRINK TO RIGHT THERE. - g

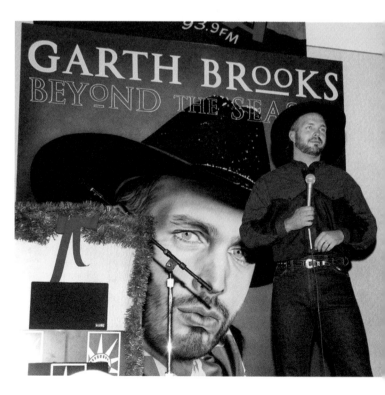

you know, lit up on the shoulder. I knew that's how this guy's going to spend Christmas Eve before going to work all day Christmas Day, and I thought, *Man, what a bummer that is.* Because Christmas is everything to me, and so it just hit me that it's just a cold shoulder he's on. I started thinking, *Wow, if we could take the listener from where they're thinking he's in this warm place, painting this nice, pleasing picture where's everything's just great, and then hit them with the truth, that it's a harsh reality, hard work, work that takes you away from your family.* I could hear those big, high harmonies. I bring it to those guys, and Kim Williams is rockin', Kent Blazy is rockin'. They are eating this up. They are spitting it out, and then in two seconds, it goes off on a different direction when I say to Kim, "You know, the first verse

WE WERE THE THREE AMIGOS, MAN, BROTHERS. **IF WE COULD HAVE WRITTEN EVERY DAY TOGETHER, WE WOULD HAVE.** - g

of this song is like when you dream of something so much but it never comes true…that what never happened is what I'll never forget feeling." And Kim Williams goes, "*What never happened is what I'll never forget.*" He goes, "Let's write that." And right then, we're in the middle of working on "Cold Shoulder," and Kent, who's supposed to be the voice of reason, goes, "Yeah, let's write that."

Kent Blazy: Now Garth would say he's the sane one. He'd blame me and Kim, you know. And then Kim would blame me and Garth, so it's, you know…

G: And so it takes us about ten minutes. We write "What Never Happened," which might have been recorded by another act, I think. Then, ten minutes after we left it, we came back to "Cold Shoulder," and by that time, the last verse, which might be one of my favorite pieces I ever got to assist writing, appeared. "This old highway's like a woman sometimes / She can be your best friend, but she's the real jealous kind / She's the lady that leads you to the life you dream of and she's the mistress that keeps you from the ones that you love." Damn, damn. If you've ever been a drinker…that's music to drink to right there.

Trisha Yearwood: This one is right up there with "New Way to Fly," maybe because I don't consider myself to be a traditional country singer, so when I get to sing on a classic country song like "Cold Shoulder," I just love it. I remember singing the last chorus straight, and then Garth asked me to try the pedal the other two voices were doing. I think Garth is really good at not overusing those choice harmonies, so it makes you want to hear more of it and how special it is. You find yourself wanting to get to that last chorus.

G: *(laughs)* I would have used that lick on every chorus, but Allen has this thing called "taste." I have never had it, never will. *(laughs again)* It was Allen who made the decision to do the bend on just the last chorus.

Trisha Yearwood: This is where Garth and Allen really think about harmonies on a song, where it needs to be and how it needs to be sung. For me, harmony enhances a song so much, the listener may not even recognize it until you go back and hear the song without the lift that harmony brings.

Kent Blazy: Garth is what I call a spewer. You kind of have to listen to him all the time. So he was over in the corner, and he was singing this other thing, and it kind of sounded bluegrass, and being from Kentucky I love bluegrass. Well, what's that? He said, "Oh, I don't know, it's just something I'm singing." I said, "Well, let's write that." In the end, it seemed this is a pretty good writing team if we can write two songs in one day. So we started writing together some and just always had a great time, the three of us.

G: "Cold Shoulder" was as country as it got. It was all a wonderful mix by Mark Miller of Trisha's high harmonies singing the *by God it's country* lyric of Kim and Kent. Blazy had a book of song titles, and we're not talking just a tablet, we're talking a book, probably 5,000 song titles in there. We'd just break out that book, and just go through there and go, "Oh, there it is right there." These guys were eating, living, and breathing music. We would talk on the phone at night, and we were the three amigos, man, brothers. If we could have written every day together, we would have.

Mark Miller: I think I was mixing it or doing a rough mix of it, and his dad, Garth's dad, was standing behind me. His dad worked in the oil business for a while, I believe, but he was a salt of the earth kind of guy, sweet guy, and he was just like, "*Ummmm.*" That one really moved him.

STILLWATER SENDOFF

Stillwater, OK, 1987 | Willie's Saloon.
The send-off party. That's Mike Sheets in the center and Randy Taylor on the right.

TRY TO IMAGINE SOME HUNDRED TO two hundred people in the town of Stillwater, Oklahoma, and they've all come together to send you off on your life's dream of going to Nashville. You've had that dream, they know it, and they want you to go after it, and, man, these people believe in you more than you know how to believe in yourself. There's a lot of love in that picture. But they don't just get together to wave when you drive off into the sunset, no, they raise all this money to make it possible. You're in the headlines of all the local papers, on the front of local magazines and stuff. What a feeling. Your hometown community shows up for you in this big way . . . and part of you realizes you're not going to do this just for yourself, you're doing it for all of them, some of those people who are never gonna leave that town. I'll never forget that.

So they send you off to Nashville, but when you get out there, it's not quite as simple as you saw it playing out in your fantasy. The town wasn't filled with straw hats and gooseneck trailers. You don't just come in and sing a couple notes for somebody and they sign you up and hand you a record deal. That wasn't what went down. And, uh, I wasn't ready for that. For like two weeks they raised money for me and . . . twenty-three hours later I was headed back home. Hell, I hid out for two weeks before they knew I was there. And I'll tell you what, when they found out I was back, no one held it over me, all they said was, "You going back?" And I said, "Yeah." And they said, "We're behind you." That's the kind of people back home in Oklahoma.

WE BURY THE HATCHET

BY ROYAL WADE KIMES AND GARTH BROOKS

Left to right: Wade Kimes, Garth, and Kent Blazy.

G: I wrote this with a guy named Wade Kimes. This kid's a cowboy out of Arkansas. He comes into the place over here, just moved in nearby, and he goes, "I got it," goes, "I got the song idea."

I said, "Well, let me hear it." He says, "We bury the hatchet, but leave the handle sticking out." I'm sitting there thinking, *This guy is the craziest guy I've ever met. There's no way it's going to work.* But we're already writing, so let's get in and write. I found myself laughing so hard, you know, your cheeks were hurting, your gut was hurting. And the groove on it was so much fun. This is the perfect example of an album cut. It sets up the rest of the album, "In Lonesome Dove" into "The River."

Even as I was writing songs, I needed to keep albums in my head, you know? I wanted every one of them to have all the ups and downs of a live show, that roller coaster. It can't be all ballads, can't be all story songs, can't be all up-tempo swing kind of stuff, just like it can't be all humor—but you damn sure need all of that stuff in its moment. So in this writing session, I'm already seeing where this can fit, what it's kind of doing to the person in the seat out there. And you can't tell me that every couple walking hand in hand through the door hasn't had a moment when they need that hand because they're reaching for the hatchet. Everybody understands this, that's for damn sure, and if you can look at it with humor, you just might survive. But then the humor, its emotion, leads us into another world, into that beautiful "In Lonesome Dove" story.

Engineer Mark Miller.

IT CAN'T BE ALL BALLADS, CAN'T BE ALL STORY SONGS, CAN'T BE ALL UP-TEMPO SWING KIND OF STUFF, JUST LIKE IT CAN'T BE ALL HUMOR— BUT YOU DAMN SURE NEED ALL OF THAT STUFF IN ITS MOMENT. - g

IN LONESOME DOVE

BY CYNTHIA LIMBAUGH
AND GARTH BROOKS

Stephanie Brown: Garth told me, before the first album came, "You're going to get a cut on this," and I didn't. Well, now after the first one, he called me and said, "Steph, you're going to get one on the next album." The next album came along and, well, again I didn't. He called me, "Hey look, I know I told you you would, but you're not going to have one on this album either." This is how it goes for songwriters, no matter the artist. But there was this song Garth would play, "In Lonesome Dove," that I just loved. I'd have him play it whenever I could. So he pacified me by saying, our song "Burning Bridges" is finally coming on the third, and it'll be on there with "In Lonesome Dove." That was *good* company.

Bob Doyle: I think that in some ways Garth has always dreamed about a particular kind of romantic hero, like the guy who catches the touchdown that wins the game but bangs his head on the goalpost and dies. *(laughs)* It's the type of story that gets you involved emotionally, in this theme of a man that sacrifices everything but may not be around when everybody else benefits from what he did. "In Lonesome Dove" has a little of that, along with a narrative that extends across generations. You know, a big story in a small space. Songs can do this like no other form.

1993 | Texas Stadium.

G: Cyndi Limbaugh comes in to Bob Doyle's office down the block. Says, "I have a letter from Larry McMurtry saying the title is just the title, feel free to write," and she does. And we write this whole little story thing and put it down on a little TASCAM four-track, and it goes on forever. The story's a hundred-years-long kind of thing. I thought, *Well, nothing will ever happen with this.* Kept it in the top drawer for a long time.

Allen Reynolds: I always liked that one as a non-single that *really* mattered to its album.

G: It's a story, yeah, but it's also a chance for the band to do their thing. They're in the studio, listening to what you're saying. You give them a narrative like this, and they can start painting these big-ass canyons and show you the color of rock. You can see the color of the sky. You know if it's dark, heavy clouds or wisps of white cloud just by the work that Milton's doing on his hardware, on the cymbals and stuff. That's really what made "In Lonesome Dove" so cool. There's a line in there, it says, "Shots rang out down the Rio Grande." Milton does this push, and he does it in such a way that it just kind of takes you to those caverns, hearing those echoes, like all the sudden you're on the Rio Grande about a mile down from where it's happening, and it's just coming to you in echoes across the water.

The receipt for the session that started it all back in Stillwater, Oklahoma, in 1987.

THESE GUYS ARE PAINTING PAINTINGS IS WHAT THEY'RE DOING. THEY'RE WORKING ON CANVAS. - g

It's so, so cool how these guys do this musical stuff that deepens the visual experience of the song. Bobby Wood does the rain, "When she saw him riding through the rain." And he does that little droplets thing off his right hand. These guys are painting paintings is what they're doing. They're working on canvas.

"YOU KNOW A DREAM IS LIKE A RIVER EVER CHANGIN' AS IT FLOWS AND A DREAMER'S JUST A VESSEL **THAT MUST FOLLOW WHERE IT GOES**"

THE RIVER

BY VICTORIA SHAW AND GARTH BROOKS

Victoria Shaw: We met at the Opryland Hotel during the Country Radio Seminar. I was just hustling my behind off trying to network and meet people and make my dreams come true. I would go there every year. I didn't pay for the seminar because it was too expensive, but, man, I hung out at that hotel every single night and made a lot of friends through the years. One night, they would have big parties in the different suites, I believe it was Westwood One Radio hosting, they had a

song that day, but it would be six months before she would write with me again, I think because she thought I was delusional. For a guy that didn't have a record deal at the time, she thought I was pretty much of a dreamer. She didn't see the lighters like I did.

Victoria Shaw: What was really interesting, though, is this boy from Oklahoma and this girl from New York and L.A. had so much in common musically. He was this huge Queen fan, and Queen was like my number one band. Elton John, Billy Joel, James Taylor. I mean, we just had a lot of music in common, so that was really fun writing with him.

> I HADN'T HAD EVEN A NOD FROM THE INDUSTRY, **BUT FOR SOME REASON WAS STUPID ENOUGH TO THINK,** OF COURSE, I'M GOING TO MAKE IT AT SOME POINT.
> - VICTORIA SHAW

G: "The River" had the word "vessel" in it, and Bob just didn't think country music would accept that. And it really bothered him, to the point where he was worried about it, which kind of made me question whether we should cut it or not. So we *don't* cut it until three years after we wrote it. Just scared to death.

party in the presidential suite, a big party. I knew Bob Doyle and Pam Lewis somehow, and we were talking and they said, "You should write with our new guy, he's over there, name's Garth Brooks." I said okay. I walked up to him and said, "Hi, I'm Victoria Shaw and I'm a friend of Bob and Pam's, and they think that you and I should write." He said, "Yes ma'am, I would like that very much." I said, "Don't call me ma'am and we'll get along just fine."

G: It was the first song I wrote with Victoria. I remember telling her, "I love where we're going with this, Vic, because I'm going to see people holding up their lighters and singing along with this." We would finish the

THIS BOY FROM OKLAHOMA AND THIS GIRL FROM NEW YORK AND L.A. **HAD SO MUCH IN COMMON MUSICALLY.**
- VICTORIA SHAW

Victoria Shaw: I tried to talk him out of the word "vessel." I thought it was an ugly word. I'm like, "Vessel?" *Come on*, that's a weird word. He's like, "No, trust me, trust me." Okay, but really *that word*. And now, as I always say, "vessel" is my favorite word, "vessel" is sending my kids to college. I try to use "vessel" in all my conversations.

Allen Reynolds: "The River," I brought that up every time we got together to work. First album, second album, and he just, he waved me off. But by the time we were cutting the third album, his brother Jerry kept asking when we were going to cut it. That might have finally prompted Garth. But, you know, it's one of those songs that are life songs as opposed to love songs. It had a mystique to it, a musicality that just sort of drew me in, and, boy, did it register with his audience out there.

Trisha Yearwood: When Garth would call you in to sing on a record, you never knew what you were getting into. Sometimes it would be something fun and raucous. Then you would find yourself singing on "The River."

Victoria Shaw: "The River" was a complete extension of where Garth and I were at the time. I mean, he didn't have an album out yet when we wrote it, so he was keeping everything, fingers and toes, crossed, dreaming big and working hard. I hadn't had even a nod from the industry, but for some reason was stupid enough to think, *Of course I'm going to make it at some point.* We were just, I always say, two wide-eyed dreamers when we wrote that song.

Trisha Yearwood: Just hearing that song for the first time and singing on it, you knew you were a part of something special. But there was no way to know how much of an anthem this song would become for so many people. What a *beautiful* message.

Uniondale, NY, 1993 | Garth and Victoria Shaw at the Nassau Coliseum .

YEAR
FOUR

1992

Funny how what you say is exactly the opposite of what you mean.
The album cover for *The Chase* is so black and white, while the music
inside is an endless shade of gray. But where do black and white
meet? They meet in the middle, and this album was all about tolerance,
courage, and self-discovery.

The photographer, Bev Parker, knew this. She studied the music, and it
was Bev who suggested the title. It's still the most personal album
I have ever been involved with. Though beaten and battered, *The Chase*
will forever be my sentimental favorite Garth Brooks album.

1992 | IMAGINE IT, you're at the top of everything you ever dreamed of, you're kind of holding it in your hands. Then *times that by ten, by twenty.* I mean, I didn't have the audacity to dream as big as what we were experiencing. But there it was. I guess what we were doing came at the right time for this beautiful audience to carry it along, for this collaboration through songs and singing and performance. And I'll tell you this, I wasn't going to watch my dreams come true just so that I could complain about how hard it was to deal with. No, sir. I was having the time of my life. Was it different? You bet.

I remember one time, *Ropin'* was out and had been for a while, and Sandy and I were at a Circuit City store in RiverGate. We're talking to a guy about a TV or something, some appliance, whatever, but Sandy looks at me and says, "Hey, will you go grab my checkbook out of the car?" I said, "Sure." It's night, and I come out of the store and I'm walking to the car, and I realize, this is the first time that I've been alone in probably two years. I am by *myself* walking to the car through a Circuit City parking lot. There is no one to the left or right of me. There is nobody that is checking my schedule. There is nobody that is leading me somewhere to do something. It was the busiest time of my life going into *The Chase,* so much so that on a simple trip to the car, all the sudden you realize, holy crap, maybe I need to get some alone time, like, hey, maybe you just need to kind of introduce yourself back to yourself.

And then, in the middle of all that, I became a parent. *The Chase* was '92, and Taylor was born in '92. Nothing is more amazing than when your child comes into the world.

Nothing. So in the middle of creating this album, this biggest of all life experiences is happening. And the crazy thing about being a parent is, the second that you hear you're one, the only thing that matters to you is ... *What is the world they live in?* That's it. What is going on outside the walls of this house that's going to affect the child inside? What's going on in the world becomes a hell of a lot more important to you. I guess that's the way God planned it, right? But as a result of all that, *The Chase* is the artist's voice for the first time. It's the first time that, I think, you really see the personality of the artist, the beliefs that are inside that person. And this is where some of the shit started to hit the fan.

This is one of the first times you started to get, "Well, Mr. Brooks, I don't share that opinion." All the sudden, Oh, okay, there's another side to this, and it's time to understand, as an artist, that there are going to be people that like your view of the world and people that don't. At shows, I'd have folks at the gate waiting for me. They had driven miles and miles to go, "Hey, man, what the hell is this?" They were very opinionated about it, as they had every right to be. But, for me, it felt like it was time to give my opinion in a song. So here comes the album of love, the album of tolerance, the album of peace, the album of confrontation, the album of communication. I got a platform, and so, with *The Chase,* I stepped up to it.

Goodlettsville, TN, 1992 | The Touring Band. Ty England (Acoustic guitar, vocals), Steve McClure (Steel and Electric guitar), Garth, David Gant (Keyboards, Vocals), James Garver (Electric guitar, vocals), Betsy Smittle (Bass, vocals), and Mike Palmer (Drums and Percussion).

WE SHALL BE FREE

BY STEPHANIE DAVIS AND GARTH BROOKS

1993 | The national anthem, Superbowl XXVII. Marlee Matlin and Garth.

G: I'm out in L.A. at the Academy of Country Music Awards. I've just come off stage after performing. I'm sharing a room with like five other artists, one of them is Travis Tritt. Travis comes in, I remember, I'm getting dressed and him going, "Boys, the whole town's burning."

Stephanie Davis: I remember right before he went out to the ACM Awards, we were sitting on a hillside by his house, writing. I don't think we had a guitar, and I was the only one that had a pen and notebook, we were just kind of having fun throwing these verses out there, tossing lines back and forth, and the hawks were flying overhead. But we didn't really know what it was we were working on.

G: The Rodney King trial was going on during that time in L.A. And, man, there was trouble out there. So, we finished the show, got on the bus, and I tell Big Jim, the bus driver, "Man, just don't stop until we have to get gas." As we pulled out of L.A., we're overlooking the city, and you could see the fires burning. Woke up at the Grand Canyon the next day, found a pay phone, called Stephanie Davis. I said, "Are you seeing what is going on out here in L.A.?"

I swear to you her exact quote was, "I'm way ahead of you." She had the title, "We Shall Be Free."

Stephanie Davis: I was back at my house in Nashville and watching these riots on TV and it was like, good God, and Garth called. I had my trusty yellow legal pad by the TV, and I was actually writing some more on it when the phone rang. He described this harrowing ride out of Los Angeles, barricades, where they barely made it, fires all around the city, and he said, "Hey, you know that song," and I said,

"I'm on it, call me when you get back to town and we'll finish it."

G: Then we met on the hill again, out at the house where we still lived, on the farm overlooking Nashville, and just started saying, "Hey man, we shall be free, when you are free to love anyone you choose, when we are all free to worship from our own kind of pew, we shall be free." And there it began.

Stephanie Davis: We came to the verse about being free to love anyone you choose. Well, this was Nashville and country radio, and I said, "Garth, are you sure we want to do this?" I was a little concerned about him, but I knew Garth had loved ones who were gay. He didn't even bat an eye. "Yeah," he says. "That's how we feel, isn't it? Let's put it in."

I REMEMBER, I'M GETTING DRESSED AND HIM GOING, **"BOYS, THE WHOLE TOWN'S BURNING."** - g

Bob Doyle: I think he's always had a strong point of view and a sense, like he knew he had a responsibility once he got up there in that position to use it properly and convey something that was important to him. I've been lucky enough to be associated with a guy that thinks like, you know, if one life changes because of the song, then he's saying it for a reason, he's singing it for a reason.

Stephanie Davis: It was one of the most exciting times, because we got it done in short order, and I think he recorded it like the next day … and I think it was on the radio the next week! Boom, boom, boom. It was really fast. At one point, I think I was working, doing some rewrites of the verses, and I'd be calling them into the studio and singing them onto the answering machine while he was downstairs cutting the tracks and stuff. It was high-pressure, which is sometimes how a diamond is made, I think.

G: I always saw the big tent revival. I always saw the big choir going. I think Stephanie originally took it a little more as a folk kind of thing. This was the first time I think I ever brought a song into the studio where I didn't have a chart or anything, and I just sang because I didn't know the chords, hadn't figured them out. So I sat with Bobby and did a little intro, like the old songs used to have, that set it up, and then the band kicked in and here we went on it.

Bobby Wood: I didn't really even pay attention to the words. I just thought, you know, my background is gospel, that's how I was raised up, and he said, "I want a gospel beginning to this song." So, again, I wasn't listening to the lyrics, I was just trying to get the music right, you know, and the feel right. We were working on the chord changes when the band came in.

G: I was raised on Mahalia Jackson. She gave me a reference point, an inspiration point. And I also had Allen Reynolds saying, "Hey, man, just communicate with me, don't try to go somewhere that isn't you, just communicate with me." I was just thinking about Mahalia Jackson's beautiful face when we were doing that vocal, and how easy she sang. I wanted to be the voice

HE DIDN'T EVEN BAT AN EYE. "YEAH," HE SAYS. **"THAT'S HOW WE FEEL, ISN'T IT? LET'S PUT IT IN."**
- STEPHANIE DAVIS

of one person in this whole mess. One voice standing beside you. I wasn't looking to be more than that. But it felt like something I needed to do.

Allen Reynolds: If you read some of the quotes from Abraham Lincoln from around the time he issues the Emancipation Proclamation, there's a real parallel to what Garth is saying here. Lincoln is talking about freeing the slaves so that we can all be free. And whether then or now, there are always people who aren't ready to receive that kind of message. Which is why there was resistance in parts of country radio. Country music radio is notoriously conservative at some level and not consistent. It's no surprise, really, that this song encountered pockets of resistance, and that's why I call it a brave song and a brave offering.

Bob Doyle: We made a video, and I'll never forget Garth spending all night trying to finish this video. The NFL said they'd air it right before the Super Bowl, and then the NFL ran into the same issues that country radio did. They were starting to slow walk us. You know, "Well, guys, I don't … we haven't got an answer as to when they'll air it," and so on. It kept going, and finally Garth said, "Well, I guess we won't sing the national anthem, so let's go." He took off his cowboy hat, put on his sweats, and we were leaving the arena, and this is getting right up to show time when he was going to sing the national anthem. They finally said, "Okay, we'll air it." I got on the phone because we didn't have mobile phones, and called a New York City bar that I knew, because I wanted to make sure the national network got it, not just locally. Then Garth went out

there and sang, and I don't think, if you watch the broadcast, they ever put the camera on Garth much at all. It was just one of those moments he sussed it out and sized it up. But he was trying to say something and wasn't going to be stopped.

Stephanie Davis: I was on tour with him. I was playing in his band then or opening shows, I can't remember. But "We Shall Be Free" had come out, and he had some threatening calls. Serious stuff, scary stuff … and I think a lesser artist would have said, "Okay, guys, we're not doing this song." But not Garth, he sang his ass off on that song. That will always stick in my mind as an image of integrity and braveness, like he means what he says and he says what he means and … it has made *me* braver. Like, if you have something to say, you say it. He gave me courage.

LEARNING FROM THE AUDIENCE

ALL I KNEW BACK when I was a kid in Oklahoma was that I loved a good song. When one of them came along, it got my attention like nothing else, went in and stayed in. It could be Merle Haggard, could be Bob Seger, Queen, George Strait, Journey, James Taylor. I just fell in love with what a good song did to me, with the way it kind of opened up inside of me. That's the first way I learned what a good song is, 'cause the good ones do that to you. But what I'd find out is that there's another way you learn which songs are the keepers, and that's when you start playing gigs, and then you learn from the best teachers out there: the audience.

I played all kinds of gigs in Oklahoma: pizza places, coffeehouses, clubs, whatever place would have us. There were the ones where I was told to play only country and the ones where I was told, "Do not play any country here." I did both kinds, and everything between. Playing shows was where what I guess you'd call my apprenticeship in performance started. Being the youngest of six, I knew how to get attention. So, in some ways, I guess I'd been studying for the job all my life. But once I was gigging, what I learned up there in front of an audience was that not all songs are equal. You'd look out on that dance floor and know what a song could do. If the bodies are leaving the dance floor, good God, don't play that one again! This is true whether you're in a fifty-person club or an arena. The audience knows, and they'll let you know.

A lot of the songs on the records got tested in front of audiences even before they got recorded. "Friends in Low Places" proved itself on the road, and to such a degree that we knew what we had going into the studio, we just had to capture it. So, yeah, the gig knows, the audience knows. You've got a question about whether a song works, take it to the people who know.

SOMEWHERE OTHER THAN THE NIGHT

BY KENT BLAZY AND GARTH BROOKS

G: This is my mom and dad's favorite song. I try not to get emotional, but that's … with them gone now it kind of hits me a little harder. But this was their song and they loved this song.

Kent Blazy: Garth and I both like to write pretty much from an idea or a title, and that day neither one of us had anything the other liked, so we kind of sat there for a little while. I had a black lab named Sophie that Garth loved. This dog was a Frisbee-playing fool, and so he said, "Let's just go out in the backyard and throw her the Frisbee." So we went out there and played with her for probably an hour or so until she finally tired out. Then we sat on a bench we had back there, and we just started talking about life and women and living and all that, and probably the whole afternoon went by, and I thought, *Well, we're not really going to get anything.* Then we went back into the house and went upstairs and got out guitars, and that song just kind of started coming out line by line.

Colleen and Raymond Brooks.

AMPEX 456

GARTH BROOKS

1) SOMEWHERE OTHER THAN THE NIGHT

HORSE OF TROY PRODUCTIONS, INC.

ITEM # A-922-0008

DESCRIPTION: SOMEWHERE OTHER THAN THE NIGHT

0233-LV-9220008

1804

PUT THAT PEN DOWN, CLOSE THAT LAPTOP. **GO TAKE A WALK WITH YOUR BUDDY.**
- g

G: It was originally written as "Sometimes You Need the Rain to See the Light." We still have the original lyrics somewhere. But what it was all about was taking time from your busy schedule to show somebody you love them. It could be your child, it could be your pet. It could be anything, just take that time, put that pen down, close that laptop. Go take a walk with your buddy. You can do that with your friends too. It's like, "Hey, man, why are we working so hard down here?"

I think it's so we can have downtime, can afford downtime with the people we love. I think that's what that song was. It just picked the farm as a vehicle to drive that message home with.

Kent Blazy: The funny thing was when we were working on the part about standing in the kitchen with nothing but an apron on, and we were trying to think, *Well, what's something really sexy we can put in there?* So, my wife was like a big Oprah fan, and I remember one show they had where they were talking about what turns your husband on. One woman said, "Well, I wrap myself in cellophane, and when he comes home from work and walks in the door, there I am and he loves that, I'm naked and standing in cellophane." And Garth said, "That actually doesn't do too much for me," and I said, "That doesn't do too much for me neither." "Well," I said, "what about standing in the kitchen with nothing but an apron on?" Of course, he loved that. That was kind of the line I think that stood out in the song, and I think it might have even helped the sale of aprons.

"HE'D COME TO REALIZE HE'D NEGLECTED CERTAIN THINGS **AND THERE ARE TIMES SHE FEELS ALONE EVEN BY HIS SIDE** IT WAS THE FIRST TIME SHE EVER SAW HIM CRY"

MR. RIGHT

BY GARTH BROOKS

G: That song was from back in Stillwater. I think we still have the original version that was actually cut back then, a little kind of a swing thing, and it was just fun. I never, ever thought we would record it for a Garth Brooks record. There were a million "Mr. Right" or "Mr. Right Now" kind of things in this town. Everybody had written that hook. I was just lucky enough to have a relationship with the artist, and so mine was the one that got cut.

Try to remember that Western swings, I would say, are like dialects, like accents. We can all be speaking English in America, but you definitely know the South from the North, you definitely know Montana from Texas. It's the same way with swing. You're going to have what we call Austin swing or San Antonio swing, which is going to have a little more of the brass added. You're going to have more Montana swing, Wyoming swing, where it is probably a little more acoustic-based music. Then you're going to have kind of like what I call an Oklahoma swing. It's a bit slicker, fewer chord variations, but it moves a little faster and a lot of it depends on harmony, some of the Sons of the Pioneers harmonies in that Oklahoma swing. It's a Western music that ran head-on into Glenn Miller and the big-band thing, with fiddles, sometimes fiddle

(Bottom) Guitarist Mark Casstevens.

WESTERN SWINGS, I WOULD SAY, ARE LIKE DIALECTS, LIKE ACCENTS.

- g

and brass, like clarinet, tenor sax. That's cowboy swing. We'd see acts come through Stillwater like Dub Cross or the Country Cousins. Dance floor would be packed.

Mark Miller: We had like these little two-step kind of songs here and there on different albums, and they're always fun 'cause when they come, the band really plays them well, making up these licks and stuff. Real fun kind of song to cut. We did this one live with fiddle and steel joining the other five guys.

G: My biggest memory of that was Mark "Crash" Casstevens came up with the opening lick, so everybody had to learn it, and I remember after that Crash walking out of here with his guitar and Mark Miller going, "Hey,

you haven't put your lick on here yet," and Casstevens turned around and said, "I didn't think I had to play it." And it took him a while. He hated it, but it was funny…he's the guy that came up with it. But he was kind of like the perfectionist, so you knew it was going to take him a while to please himself. Probably played it a hundred times, and with each attempt, we were all blown through the roof, but he had to get it just right. Music matters to Crash.

Chris Leuzinger: Garth thought that *everybody* should play it, bass, fiddle, steel, everybody, so there's Mark packing up his guitar…*Wait a minute*, come back here!

Allen Reynolds: *(laughs)* That lick *sounds* like Mark, too.

EVERY NOW AND THEN

BY BUDDY MONDLOCK AND GARTH BROOKS

Every Now + then

Drums: Milton Sledge
Bass: Mike Chapman
Keyboards: Bobby Wood
Acoustic Gtrs. Mark
        Casstevens
Electric + Got String Gtrs,
Chris Leuzinger

Chris Leuzinger

G: When I came to town and met Bob Doyle, Bob let me know that he planned on resigning from ASCAP and starting a publishing company himself. He couldn't approach me until he had resigned from ASCAP, but when he did, he said, "I've got you and one other writer, a guy named Buddy Mondlock."

Buddy Mondlock was an artist out of Chicago that was more folky. He had a cool sound, made some records by himself up in Chicago.

Bob Doyle: There were two kids when I started, Garth and a guy named Buddy Mondlock. You'll see Buddy's name on some of these songs, and Buddy is a very talented folk writer who I met through Guy Clark.

G: I loved Buddy Mondlock. Love him to this day, as an artist and as a person. When we first met, I was working at the boot store, Cowtown Boots, and I kind of write this poem, again, based on a past relationship in my life. I write this poem and call Buddy.

ALLEN WAS ALWAYS GOOD ABOUT LETTING US HAVE THAT ONE MORE ROLL, ONE MORE PASS TO TRY SOMETHING OUT.
- CHRIS LEUZINGER

Buddy Mondlock: Apparently it was a slow day at the store, and Garth had written some verses where the narrator was thinking about an old girlfriend. He read them to me over the phone, and I wrote them down. I really liked it, because the guy in the song acknowledged the real connection they'd had but without wishing he had her back again. He was happy with his life now.

It was just the words at that point, so after we hung up I got my guitar out and started fooling around with a melody and then added a little B section based on what we'd talked about.

G: I've never ever turned anything over to anybody like that, but I turned it over to him. Buddy does all the music, adds a bridge. I was so happy with what I got back.

Buddy Mondlock: A couple of days later we played it for Bob Doyle, and he suggested one small change. We'd written, "I love my wife and I'd never trade between what you and me had and the life I've made." Bob said, "Why don't you say, 'I love my life' instead of, 'I love my wife.' It'll be more universal."

Chris Leuzinger: Some of my favorite cuts we ever did are on *The Chase*. I particularly love that song "Every Now and Then." We used to really work hard . . . well, not work hard but

concentrate on finding little inner workings and musical things, *(laughs)* stuff that would be cool and give some kind of layers to a track. You can hear Mark Casstevens and me finding this kind of thing on here.

Allen Reynolds: We were here overdubbing with Chris, and we'd tried some other things on that song that just weren't, weren't quite working. Finally Chris came in, and I was talking to him and saying to him, "I think we've got it. I don't think we need to worry about it anymore, we're okay." He said, "Well, there's just one other thought I had and that's I could try a gut string on here." And I went, "Oh, yeah," *(laughing)* "I'd love to hear that."

So, he came back out and played gut string on it and I loved it. And then the record really was finished. You have to give the song the space and time to become a record, let the ideas flow freely.

Chris Leuzinger: Allen was always good about letting us have that one more roll, one more pass to try something out, as long as there were tracks available.

G: In the live shows, when people bring out their signs, I get a ton of "Every Now and Then" out there. It's just one of those songs, and one of my favorite songs to sing.

WALKIN' AFTER MIDNIGHT

BY ALAN BLOCK AND DONN HECHT

This is my mom, Colleen, during her recording career.

G: My mother was drop-dead gorgeous. The pictures, I mean, she was a model. It was just crazy. The girl had it all in one package. When we were growing up, she'd talk about the people she sang with, like Jackie Gleason, 'cause she loved performing with orchestras. She called it pop, but there was stuff she did that was stone country. And my mom sang with Patsy Cline at the *Louisiana Hayride*. So that was my mom's kind of music. And she would have treated "Walkin' After Midnight" the way her son did.

Chris Leuzinger: You have "Walkin' After Midnight" and "We Shall Be Free," that's like worlds apart, stylistically. And, once again, Garth is nailing it in both arenas. He was the reason we could go so wide musically without it ever seeming like we were straying. As a singer, there was a lot he could do and still be himself.

G: There was a very Patsy kind of feel to the vocal treatment on "Walkin' After Midnight," because I always thought Patsy had a very, I don't want to say masculine, but she was a strong female with a mid-range that could compete with any man. I always enjoyed that about her singing, and I always thought it made her unique, because she was maybe the strongest female voice that I ever heard in my life. Thinking about another voice that is like that, it's got to be Trisha Yearwood. Just that, what I call that thick chocolate milk, just velvety with muscle and strength. So, for me, this song transferred over well to a male singer.

> # YOU HAVE "WALKIN' AFTER MIDNIGHT" AND "WE SHALL BE FREE," THAT'S LIKE WORLDS APART, STYLISTICALLY.
> ## - CHRIS LEUZINGER

Allen Reynolds: That's just one of the country classics that reminded us where Garth comes from. He always wants to stretch out, but he never loses contact with home.

G: Mom played the *Hayride*, but she also played the *Ozark Jubilee*, all those things that were around Arkansas and Oklahoma. There would be big artists that were on the bill coming through at the time, doing those events, and she'd be on the same shows with them. Mom didn't ever seem to be starstruck that much, and she was very confident in her own singing. Just listening to her records, as an outsider, even though I'm her son, I'd say she should have been confident, because I'd put her in the top five female vocalists I've ever heard in my entire life. She was fabulous. I guess doing "Walkin' After Midnight" kind of brought me closer to her world. And that was a good place to be. Then and now.

THE DEMO SINGERS

Trisha Yearwood and Garth.

WHEN A NASHVILLE songwriter feels like they've got a good song on their hands, a lot of times they'll record a demo, something artists looking for material can listen to. Artists get to know what's out there by checking out these demos, and there are song pluggers and publishers looking to get material into the artists' hands, to get that stuff recorded. There's kind of a system to it all, a Nashville thing. Trisha Yearwood and I were both working as demo singers before we got record deals. Songwriters would hire you for sessions, and you'd go in and cut a batch of their songs. Or a few songwriters would get together and share the cost of putting a session together. And it wasn't just us doing this work, there were folks like Martina McBride and Faith Hill, Joe Diffie, Linda Davis—names you know. It was a way to get in front of a mic, hone your craft and help you do your own thing.

Trisha got to be the first-call female singer for demo sessions. Just singing on everybody's sessions. She'd been a secretary at MTM Records, Mary Tyler Moore's label, but left because she was so busy with the demo work. We both got to know a lot of musicians, a lot of writers, so many people, through singing on demos. It was a great time in our lives. Best of all, we got to know each other. It was Kent Blazy who made it happen.

Kent kept telling me he wanted me to meet Trisha, but I had a female singer I'd been working with and kind of wanted to honor that relationship. But Kent kept at it, and finally he puts together a session for us to do a duet. He was convinced that our voices would really work together, you know, just thinking musically. I'll never forget that day, sharing a microphone for the first time. The way our voices worked together. That day would turn out to have the biggest impact on my music and in my life.

DIXIE CHICKEN

BY LOWELL GEORGE AND MARTIN KIBBEE

Allen Reynolds: "Dixie Chicken" may have been inspired by his thoughts about the performances and what he needed out there. Garth was always thinking about the live show. With this one, I think he had a good sense for how people would respond to it, and, sure enough, he had enormous amounts of fun doing it for an audience. I'm guessing that's what prompted him to record it. But, again, I certainly had no problems with it because it has such a good feel with this band.

G: I didn't know the song. I was way behind on this one. I remember, in fact, I'd just been signing autographs in Florida, and I get on the bus from signing. I'm getting undressed, and in that spot in Florida there was this kind of embankment that you had to drive out of, so it was pretty steep. It was like trying to stand up when an airplane is taking off kind of thing, you're kind of leaning, and I've got the music playing already. I already had my headphones on. And I hear "Dixie Chicken," from Little Feat. I'm thinking, *Holy cow, this is good.* "Dixie Chicken" had to have come out in the early seventies, just such a rich time in music.

Trisha Yearwood: I just remember Little Feat being funky and cool. And this was a chance for me to be funky. *(laughs)* Allen and Mark always mixed my vocal on Garth records really loud. I would joke about it, but inside I was so proud to be that prominent in the final mix.

G: Mark would mix Trisha's vocals up so loud in all the records. I remember asking him, "Do you think Trisha's harmony is loud on this mix?" He went into this dazed stupor and uttered, "Yes…isn't it wonderful?"

Bobby Wood: Yeah, I thought that was a pretty funky, funky track. I thought it was a new song when we recorded it because I had never heard it. I didn't listen to radio. I was working so much back in those days, if I wasn't writing I was in the studio. But that one felt *good* when we got on it.

THEY TOOK TO THIS LIKE DUCKS TO WATER, MAN. **THIS WAS EVERY KIND OF MUSIC THAT THEY WERE BORN TO PLAY.**
- g

G: Wherever we're going from Florida, I'm replaying that thing—I probably have a Discman—and I musta put it on repeat, hearing it maybe fifty, sixty times driving back, going, *This is a great sing-along and this would be fun.* And the band would love it too. It sure worked for this five-piece ensemble, I can tell you that. They took to this like ducks to water, man. Then add Rob's fiddle, Bruce's lap slide, and Trisha's harmony, and this was every kind of music that they were born to play…all in one record!

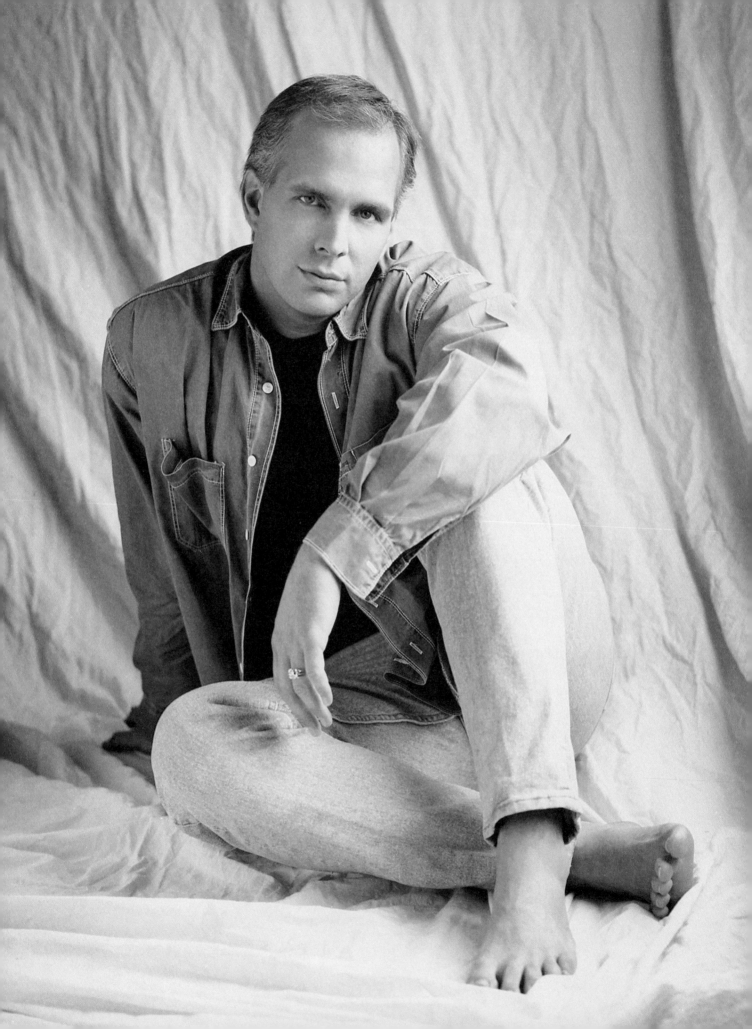

LEARNING TO LIVE AGAIN

BY DON SCHLITZ AND STEPHANIE DAVIS

Stephanie Davis: This was something I'd heard a guy say when I was playing in some bar band, can't remember where. This really big guy, probably three hundred pounds, just before he sat down at this table and passed out, he said, "This learning to live again is killing me." Then his head hit the table and he was out. I was just haunted by that line, and so I remembered it, carried it with me for a while.

G: *Whew.* Talk about the sign we see a lot, that's everywhere when we're playing live and doing the housekeeping part of the show, "Learning to Live Again." Of the stuff we don't do during the regular show, that's the one you see requested more than anything else out there. The audience knows it inside and out. They'll sing it along with you like they do "Unanswered Prayers." Beautiful, beautiful thing.

Stephanie Davis: By then I was writing for EMI, and they'd set me up with a writing partner, Don Schlitz, kind of a Nashville legend.

1989 | Garth and Stephanie Davis.

TAPE LEGEND

Jack's Tracks
RECORDING STUDIO INCORPORATED

white jacket

1308 16th Ave. So., Nashville, Tennessee 37212 – (615) 385-2555

Date: 5/5/92

ARTIST	LABEL	PRODUCER	DATE	STUDIO	ENGINEER	REEL #	PURCHASE ORDER #	TAPE		NOTES
GARTH BROOKS	LIBERTY	ALLEN REYNOLDS	TUES. PM		MARK MILLER			TYPE: 456 AMPEX LEVEL: +5/200 SPEED: 30 IPS		

1	2	3	4	5	6	7	8	9	10	11	12	13	14	15	16	17	18	19	20	21
TIME: 3:50		MASTER #			TITLE: DIXIE CHICKEN							REMARKS		Donna McElroy - Yvonne Hedges Vicki Hampton - Debbie Nims				2nd vs. "WINE" → 1st of Repeat Ch		
ELEC GTR 5Y5	BASS	KICK	SNA	HAT	L	R	VOICES GUYS - LAST CHO	① LINE HARM 3RD VS.		ELECTRIC CHRIS L.		PIANO B. WOOD		VOICES		FIDDLE Rob	SLIDE Bruce	VOC FIX ★	VOC ★ MAIN	ACOUST MARK CAS

BRING UP IN LICK 3/4 VS. (LEVEL'S DOWN)

1	2	3	4	5	6	7	8	9	10	11	12	13	14	15	16	17	18	19	20	21
TIME: 10:37		MASTER #			TITLE: LEARNING TO LIVE AGAIN							REMARKS		(ONLY)				LAST CHORUS "SHE J...		
ELEC GTR 5Y5	BASS	KICK	SNA	HAT	L	R		STRINGS (W/OH 23)		ELECTRIC		PIANO		KEYBOARD		STEEL SOLO ★	STEEL MAIN ★	VOC FIX ★	VOC ★ MAIN	ACOUS

Now, I'm not much of a co-writer, but I thought, *Well, gosh, I'd love a chance to write with Don Schlitz.* So I brought that title in, and we worked it up pretty shortly. It was kind of funny, though, because, I mean, we had a style. That was about the only song we wrote together, and we were…it was kind of contentious, really. We were batting it back and forth. I think people were standing outside the door wondering if they should call 911 the way we were going at it. And he was hospitalized the next day with hives. *(laughs)* So we never wrote again. Truth is, he's a great guy. I just saw him a little while ago. He's amazing, and he's truly one of the true craftsmen.

G: I just love the realness of it, that, *Oh my God, I've forgotten her name.* Because the truth is, man, you're thinking of everything except where you're at right at that time. You're still thinking about how you could have saved what you lost. You're wondering what the person you lost is doing right now. You're stupidly scared to death that who you lost is going to walk in and see you with this other person, and half of you is hoping that they do. It's a crazy time in your life if you've ever gone through it. And we all have, in some way. And this song just gets it.

Stephanie Davis: What I absolutely loved, and moved to Nashville for, were the killer story songs. When I got here, I had a chance to meet a few of those writers of the generation I grew up hearing, and that was worth everything. Hank Cochran and people like that. A great story song is deceptively simple, you know, you think, *Oh, I could write that.* But that conversational tone, telling something with a twist at the end, it's a formula but it isn't at all. It has to come from some real living. Songwriters are my favorite people on earth. The people that write those songs, they're quirky and not perfect, and half of them have been married five times and gone up and down and all around, and I love that. I think Hank Cochran moved and left Nashville three different times, and each time was an interesting story, as interesting as his songs. I just loved that part of the town. With "Learning to Live Again," Garth asked just one thing of me, and that's that he wanted to change the names from

THEN IT BECAME EVEN MORE REAL FOR ME. AND I COULD REALLY SEE IT, AND BECAUSE OF THAT, *REALLY* SING IT. - g

Gracie and Dave to Debbie and Charlie, after his friends Debbie and Charlie Stefl. He did that because he wanted it to be real to him.

G: Any chance you get to make somebody else's song yours, you take it. So, for me, in the opening verse, Debbie and Charlie were not a part of the original lyrics. Debbie and Charlie comes from my friends Debbie and Charlie Stefl. But all the sudden, when you brought in my Debbie and Charlie, you could see their faces when you sang it, and it kind of sets the song in a place and time, kind of gives you that reality to work with. It was real stuff, then it became even more real for me. And I could really see it, and because of that *really* sing it.

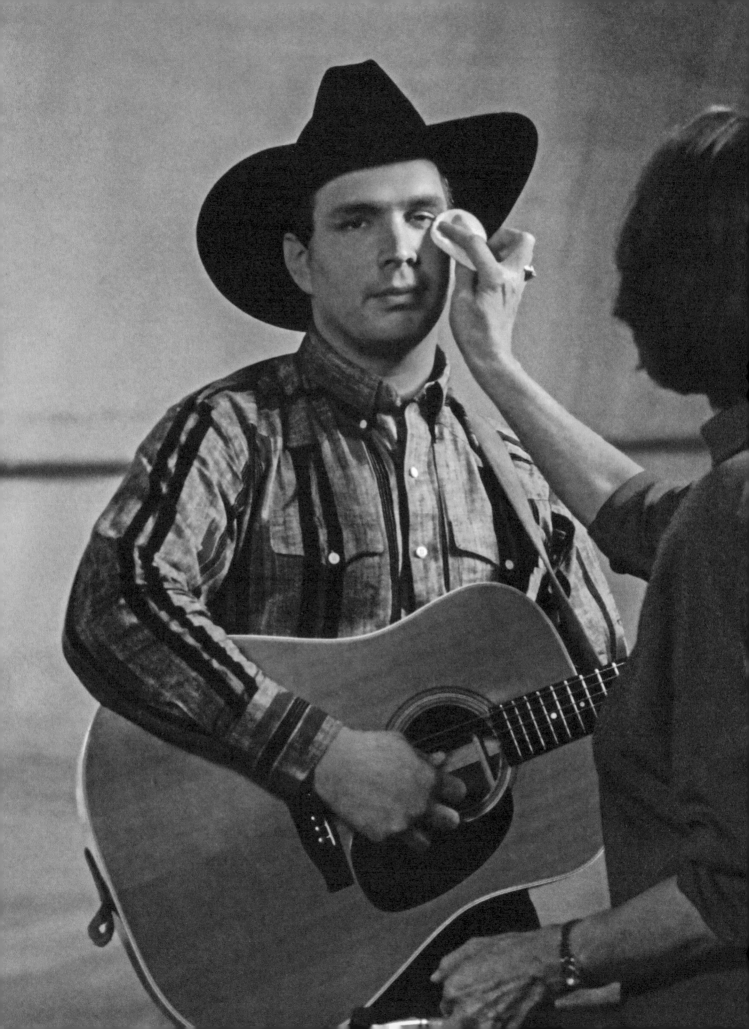

"SHE'S ASKED ME TO DANCE, **NOW HER HAND'S IN MINE** OH, MY GOD, I'VE FORGOTTEN HER NAME"

THAT SUMMER

BY PAT ALGER, SANDY MAHL
AND GARTH BROOKS

Pat Alger: Those other songs I wrote with Garth were written before he was Garth Brooks. He was just Garth from Oklahoma. Then, a year or so later, he's Garth Brooks, and we try to write "That Summer," and suddenly we're really sweating bullets and working when he has time, because he's gotten so busy. I loved the idea of the song, though, because, once again, I drew on something similar that happened to me in college, not exactly the same. I had a big love crush on an older woman, and she was a really important person to me at that particular moment in my life.

G: I love the song simply because it talks about great sex with two people that share a fantastic moment, with no regrets and no hesitation. And it kind of fills the needs of both partners, in two different ways, but completes the puzzle in one tremendous way.

Pat Alger: So when we started talking about the thing, you know a lot of that personal experience

1991 | Pat Alger and Garth.

kind of came out. We wrote that song pretty quickly again, like we did the others, but when he played it for Allen, Allen just didn't like it.

G: He hated it. *(laughs)*

Pat Alger: So we went back at it. There's a lot of lyrics, if you notice in that song. But we rewrote the lyrics, kind of made it a slightly different song…and he didn't like it much better then. He said, "You guys really need to go back and think about what you're trying to say here," so we wrote it one more time.

G: When we went back upstairs to start writing again, I told Pat about my high school girlfriend who was everything to me—she was a senior, I was a junior—and a summer we spent in the wheat fields of Oklahoma.

IT'S THE GEOGRAPHY OF OKLAHOMA, THAT'S WHAT IS JUST SO PRESENT IN THAT SONG. **THE WHEAT FIELDS AS FAR AS YOU CAN SEE AND THE BIG SKY.**
- ALLEN REYNOLDS

I FIND MYSELF
THE SAME WAY AS THE
CROWD,
**HUNGERING
FOR IT
AND LOVING IT.** - g

Allen Reynolds: It's the geography of Oklahoma, that's what is just so present in that song. The wheat fields as far as you can see and the big sky. I think it's part fantasy, part fact, right out of Garth's background.

Pat Alger: I think Allen trusts his artists, really to the point where he's going to go along with anything he can. But sometimes, not often, he gives this kind of feedback. I think what he was trying to say to us, and I think he was right, was that the earlier version was just a little too explicit, it was a little less about the whatever you want to call it, the emotional part, it was more about the physical part. And he was absolutely right, as he almost always was about everything I ever talked to Allen Reynolds about. He was almost always right because he's such a good writer himself. I mean, that was one of the fortunate things that Garth had going for him, he had a great producer who was one of the great songwriters of all time helping him pick songs. Those albums are crammed full of really interesting songs. They're some great fun songs, story songs, ballads, there's variety, but they're *all* written at a very high level.

G: "That Summer" is one of those songs where the verses put so much pressure on the chorus to deliver, that chorus had to be screaming. I have always said it was Trisha pulling double duty on the choruses that made this song fly.

Trisha Yearwood: Garth asked me to sing both parts because the third was too high for him. So on the record, I am doing my best Garth impersonation and then I added the higher harmony. Trust me, those harmonies were not easy to sing.

G: I was doing something for a company, and I can't remember what company it was, but it's somewhere around 2000, and they let a publicist kind of talk about the music, and the publicist had this line: "We all remember

where we were the first time we heard 'That Summer' and what it meant to us individually." It threw me for such a loop, because of all the songs, I think that's probably the one that gets the biggest response that I never ever guessed it would. Just surprised me. But "That Summer" might be one of the top three or four songs in the live show now, one that people just hunger for and wait for. When we first started playing it, it was just the young guys. They loved "That Summer." But now I find women's reaction to that song is what's surprising me. It's also the music that drives that thing. I find myself the same way as the crowd, hungering for it and loving it. When we did the Hall of Fame, when I was lucky enough to go in, Bob Seger showed up and played "That Summer." They got the three guys that I wrote the songs for, so George Straight sang "Much Too Young," James Taylor sang "The River," and Bob sang "That Summer." It was a perfect night for me.

FACE TO FACE

BY TONY ARATA

Tony Arata: I can't name you any other artist that would take a shot on that song. Just getting that out there on the table.

G: *Whew!* "Face to Face." So Tony Arata has this song and it is pretty damn scary, especially "the Devil ain't in the darkness, he's a rattling around inside." That's something that most of us can't admit. We just can't. We sure as hell don't *want* to, but it's like anything else, if you respect the snake, you aren't going to get bitten by him. It's when you don't is when he'll jump up and grab you.

Tony Arata: We were all standing on the balcony steps at the ASCAP Awards, getting ready to have a picture taken of all the writers who'd had number one hits that year. And Garth starts singing "Face to Face" to me. Just some of the lines from the song. I don't think it had even been recorded yet. Soon after that he calls me and asks if I would consider adding a verse.

1990 | Left to right: Dennis Morgan, Tony Arata, Don Tolle, and Tom Long at the #1 party for "The Dance."

FROM "WE SHALL BE FREE" TO "FACE TO FACE," THERE'S A THREAD IN THERE. **I THINK IT'S SELF-DISCOVERY.** - g

G: For me, it was missing one more layer. It went from a child to an adult really quick in the song, and so I told Tony, I said, "Can you write another verse to this, something about where a child is forced to be an adult too soon?"

I didn't even know what I was asking. He came back with the date rape verse. Just so powerful. This guy just kills me. You can't follow a song like that, that's why it's the last one.

Tony Arata: He settled on the verse that he did because I remember talking to him, telling him that if you look at the verses, the way they're formatted, there's certain elements involving the hand that had to be in each one. The kid finally makes it good with the bully. The nonbeliever finally prays with his

hands. And the added verse had something like, "with a finger you can put his fists away." Details, but important details to the song.

G: From "We Shall Be Free" to "Face to Face," there's a thread in there. I think it's self-discovery, I really do. I think the greatest battles that we will ever have are within, and what is the thing that can get there? Music. Music is the only thing that you let that deep in your soul. Music lets you sing with the other voice that you hear your whole life, in your head and in your heart and in your chest. My dad called it "the little man inside" when we were kids. It gives you your conscience, your comfort, your platform, your fun, your voice. Music's like someone to sing along with and talk to throughout your whole life.

1990 | Left to right: David Gant, Ty England, Mike Palmer, Garth, Steve McClure, James Garver, and Tim Bowers.

YEAR FIVE
1993

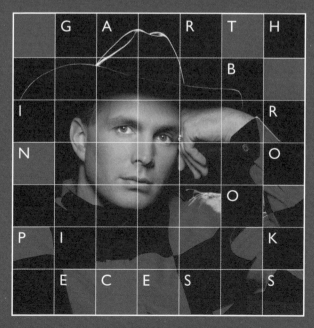

GARTH BRINOOKS PIECES

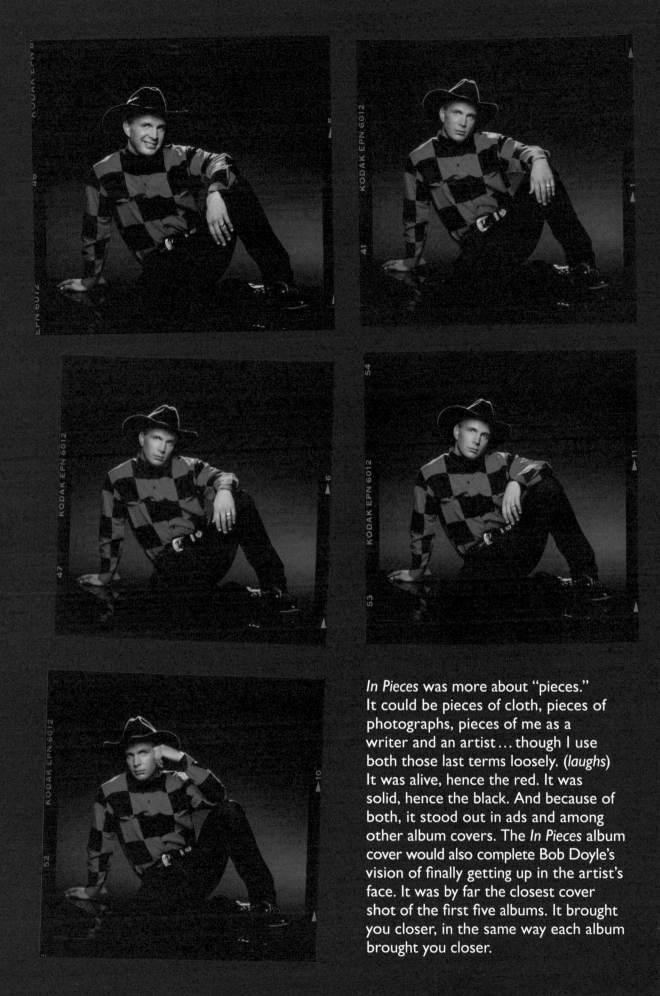

In Pieces was more about "pieces." It could be pieces of cloth, pieces of photographs, pieces of me as a writer and an artist…though I use both those last terms loosely. *(laughs)* It was alive, hence the red. It was solid, hence the black. And because of both, it stood out in ads and among other album covers. The *In Pieces* album cover would also complete Bob Doyle's vision of finally getting up in the artist's face. It was by far the closest cover shot of the first five albums. It brought you closer, in the same way each album brought you closer.

1993 | WHEN WE WOULD leave the studio, Mark Miller or Allen Reynolds would always, without fail, walk you out and make sure you got to your car, because, you know, at that time there were people being shot on 16th Avenue. So they always used to walk me to my car. One day, Mark Miller was at my side and we were talking about albums. We were talking about what they do, kind of what an album can be for that person listening. We'd always had more time to think about these kind of things, about what we were doing, and now, because we were so damn busy, it was a matter of making albums in your available time. So that bigger question: *What is an album?* Well, that was something we needed to make time for.

Walking me out that day, Mark Miller says, "An album reveals who that artist is at the time they are making the album, and you're going to have to give a piece of yourself in every song." And there it was, just like that. Here comes Garth Brooks's *In Pieces*. It just made all kinds of sense. It was an idea that tied that whole record together, because, come on, this might be the most *diverse* record that we ever cut, even with the stuff later on. You're going to pair "The Cowboy Song" with "Ain't Goin' Down ('Til the Sun Comes Up)." You're going to put "Calling Baton Rouge" on there, and right after is a song called "The Night Will Only Know," which to this day we can't figure out what the beat is on it, if it's a samba or what it is. But you've got some material that comes down the middle, right along with some really out-there stuff.

As an album, it's a roller coaster. There's more of the live show's energy in it than ever before. But our lives were also roller coasters, with things at the height of craziness, unbelievable visibility, just…you couldn't turn on a TV without seeing yourself. You couldn't open a magazine or a newspaper without reading about it. And there were opinions about everything.

I mean, "One Night a Day" is on there, and it's got a sax solo. This was a single for us, but one of the radio stations was having trouble playing it, or justifying playing it, saying "This could be on a Billy Joel record." You know, so these guys are worried at that point if it was country enough. And I was like, "Whatever." For me, the *artist* is country, so whatever he does, well, that's country. A funny time. You were sitting in extreme highs and extreme lows, and the only thing that stayed constant was the music, was that set list. Thank God and Allen Reynolds. Because what's coming next is…we brought it to a boiling point here in the States…now, let's take it to the world.

STANDING OUTSIDE THE FIRE

BY JENNY YATES AND GARTH BROOKS

Allen Reynolds: Garth had always wanted a mix of songs, from that first record forward. Some songs he'd be a writer on, some would come from outside writers. So, for me, as producer, a constant occupation was to find some of that outside material, to find songs. The further you go, of course, the harder that is, because you're wanting to bring something fresh and something a little different.

By *In Pieces*, it was a whole lot of work, just because of the volume of material that was coming through the door. Per week I'd listen to maybe three large grocery bags full of cassettes. I would work all day here at the studio, go home at night, get stoned, and sit down and start listening to tapes, listening until I was about ready to fall over. I had people handing me tapes in restaurants, department stores. I have been handed songs at the urinal. *(laughs)* So help me God, that's the truth.

1993 | Texas Stadium.

Mark Miller: When someone slides you that tape of their song, that's called "the Nashville Handshake."

Allen Reynolds: I felt like, *Hey, if somebody takes the trouble to bring this song, I have to listen to it, because it might be the most fantastic thing that ever walked through the door.* I came here as a songwriter, I've got a soft spot for them. And I've always taken the position that this, the song, is our lifeblood, and I'm the contact point for this artist. I can't slack off. But it gets tougher and tougher to stay fresh.

G: Well, this thing just kept building. It's not like the first three records go away when you make your fourth and fifth. Your new ones just add a layer of energy to this growing, what would you call it…*force.* Just pure momentum. But now, we are *never* home, but I still need to keep writing, trying to do that thing Bob Doyle

G: This was the first one that Jenny and I had out there as writers. I'd written with her before, but, you know, there are so many different kinds of writers that fit with me, each one brings something different, and Jenny's moment really came with *In Pieces*. She was a little different, because it was once she left the writing session that she really went to work. Back then, we had faxes, and she'd send you fifteen, twenty pages of fax that would go from top to bottom of the song, and not one line was exactly the same as the one you got before that. I'd go through and circle, like…*Oh, I love that line, love what that says, love this, love that,* then put all of the stuff together. She's a workhorse, and her well is infinite. That's what you want in a songwriting partner.

Jenny Yates: In those days, I'd say a word, and he'd say, "What does that mean?" I'd look it up in the dictionary and read it to him.

WHEN SOMEONE SLIDES YOU THAT TAPE OF THEIR SONG, THAT'S CALLED "THE NASHVILLE HANDSHAKE."
- MARK MILLER

told me from the start: write songs, write songs, write songs. That meant finding collaborators on the road, as well. Here comes the West Coast writer Jenny Yates.

Jenny Yates: Garth said he was coming to California, Los Angeles, and asked if I would like to get together. I said yes. Then I got a call asking if I could meet him for breakfast the next day. We started talking, and he was describing something that just "stood outside the fire" for him. Both of us instantly recognized we had an idea to work on.

He wanted to hear all of the meanings. I recall the word "abide" really opened up and helped us find our bridge.

Trisha Yearwood: What made Garth different as an artist was his ability and his desire to evolve and to take some chances and some risks. I think there is a comfort in staying with the same kind of songs, you know that's what works and you know that radio is going to like a certain song, a certain theme. But songs like "We Shall Be Free" were certainly going to test the waters. This guy is not just going to

sing swing tunes and the occasional ballad. I think "Standing Outside the Fire" also took it another leap. As a song it's very inspirational, but, in my mind, it's probably the one song that is the clearest description of who Garth is.

To me, that song's about really living rather than merely surviving. You've got to get in there to really see what can happen. I think that's who he is and who he has always been. But you put that song on the same album with "American Honky-Tonk Bar Association" and you can get away with it. He's a true album maker—these are *collections* of songs.

G: This one was a statement I felt like I needed to make, maybe because it was also a statement I needed to hear. You know, it's one of those songs about living, about taking those risks, those chances, not playing it safe, *allowing* failure, allowing a little mess along the way. What is it they say, "Better to fail trying than to never try"? If we don't respond to passion— to that thing deep within us—are we really living the fullest life? And I've always believed that. And throughout my life, *songs* have been the things that have helped me remember that. This song joined that family. And once we brought it in the studio, it got a treatment that was different from anything we'd ever done.

Some people didn't know what to think of that percussion, called it…you know, "Here's Garth Brooks with the African Mamba Tribe" and stuff, *(laughs)*—but that song, that song was just too strong and the message was too universal and global to let go of. And I gotta tell you, like, say, "That Summer," "Standing Outside the Fire" is a bigger song today than it was when we released it. It didn't just last, it *grew*. It was one of the tracks from *In Pieces* that just brought something special to the live shows, and the audience never let go.

(Bottom) Producer Allen Reynolds.

193

"LIFE IS NOT TRIED, IT IS MERELY SURVIVED IF YOU'RE STANDING OUTSIDE THE FIRE"

THE NIGHT I CALLED THE OLD MAN OUT

BY PAT ALGER, KIM WILLIAMS AND GARTH BROOKS

Pat Alger: I think it's almost like something from the folk tradition rather than rock or country. I feel like Garth has these songs that give you the feeling they've been around a long time before they were recorded, like they come from some trunk full of great songs that he got his hands on.

Allen Reynolds: I think he's real visual, Garth. More than I am. I think he just sees songs as well as hears them, and that's something I've noticed all the way through. And I think it gives him tremendous strength as a songwriter and a singer. You can put yourself in these scenes.

G: Being the last of six kids, I saw some things, I'll tell you that much. I was in this dining room, I was there that night the room fell silent, at least a few times. *(laughs)* I was smart enough to never call my dad out, or I'd just *seen* enough, being the youngest, to know where this stuff went. My dad was seventy years old and on oxygen and I wouldn't fuck with him. He was a loving guy, but he could answer the bell. I never saw him *not* answer the bell. Yeah, man, you watched your older brothers and, no shit, I watched them crawl, not because he made them, just because their own pride wouldn't let them stand up. You know, when you're a kid, you're a child watching this, it's scary, but it was how that generation settled disputes.

Bob Doyle: His dad was in the Marine Corps, was a Golden Gloves boxer, so he could really box. It wasn't like Garth's brothers were going up against just anyone.

G: What I don't know as a young man is that for this house to go on with a leader,

Dad playing the old Gibson guitar all of us kids learned how to play guitar on.

that leader sometimes needs to show *why* he's the leader. But I want to make sure you understand that I'm not defending my father or taking a position, I'm just telling you how it was. There was democracy in our house. My dad was really open. In fact, I was amazed how open he was to people's opinions that he didn't share. The problem wasn't a difference of opinion, it was disrespect. That's when the red flag kind of came up. Then he just couldn't go backward anymore.

Chris Leuzinger: When Garth would come and present songs like this to us, they were such cool songs—real stories, you know, songs with a real strong story line. You could think outside the box for the guitar part, almost more theatrically, visually, like you're part of a team building this set for a movie.

G: If you notice the very opening *(hums song)*, there's all that up-tempo, almost frantic musical movement, and that, to me, is everything that goes on in that moment of thinking, *Fuck man, just say you're sorry. That's all you got to do. Just*

say you're sorry. But for some reason, everything is just moving so fast, you're not going to say you're sorry. You know, but what my dad always did, he just went until the kid stopped. Always. Just until they stopped. He didn't want this to go one second longer than it needed to go.

Pat Alger: I think we all had a hand in that song, but the guy that made that one work would definitely be Garth.

Allen Reynolds: I think the audience wants to know what makes the artist tick, what the artist thinks and feels, and an album is a chance to really reveal some of that. Not all, but some. Jack Clement said one of his tips for songwriters was: "Reveal some of yourself in all of your songs." He said he'd started to say, "Reveal yourself in all of your songs," and then thought, *There's no sense in telling the friends and neighbors everything,* so he changed it to "some." *(laughs)* But Garth? He shares a lot of himself, and it brings a lot of truth to the material.

AMERICAN HONKY-TONK BAR ASSOCIATION

BY BRYAN KENNEDY AND JIM RUSHING

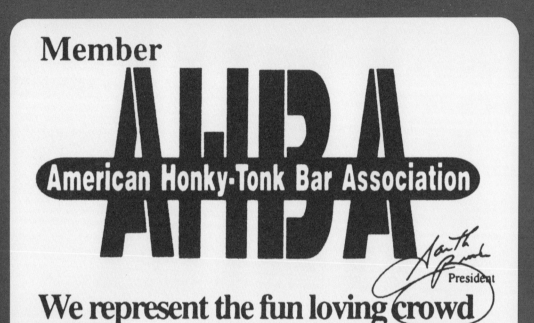

G: Believe me, we were having fun with this one. I remember asking the writer's permission to make a change to the lyrics. I wanted that "bare crack" line in there, wanted to kind of take it to another place. That plumber's crack, man, it's those guys that are always working, and I'm one of them. Every guy is one of them in some way. You get in one of those positions where it's, *Oh, my God*, and you don't know what's showing somewhere back there because you're either under a car, under a sink or something, and it's part of who we are. This song was the party song of the workforce, which made it a joy to do. It was one of those songs that you just kept playing in your truck. Bryan Kennedy had sent me probably three or four things, and I chose "AHBA" because I thought a particular voice could come through on that, a voice that's important to who I am as an artist.

Bryan Kennedy: Jim Rushing and I start every songwriting session just ... just talking about stuff. That day, the conversation turned to specific groups of people, and it seemed every group seemed to be labeled somehow. There was an acronym for this, for that, a special group here, another one there. I'd spent my early years working on a farm in West Nashville while trying to get a writing deal. So Jim and I began discussing the thoughts of the "hardworking man or woman" not having a group. Jim brought up the "bar association," and there it was. "If your paycheck depends on the weather and the clock" ... that group. And the song was born.

G: I knew there would be people who were gonna hear that and think, *Finally, yes, we're back to Garth Brooks*, just like there would be other people that would say, "How can you sing 'We Shall Be Free' and 'AHBA' at the same show?" My answer to that was always, "Guys, we can

1994 | Dan "Rodeo" Roberts, Dave Roberts, Garth, and Bryan "Chuck" Kennedy.

love one another, but at the same time we all need to pull our own weight." When you're down, put your hand out, we'll reach down to help pull you back up, but none of us want to be carried, we want to contribute.

It's like there's a thing in raising children, you want to do everything for them, but at the same time they are never going to gain that feeling of accomplishment, success, and empowerment within their own world if they don't do it themselves. And that's a tough, tough line to walk right there, because you love them so much. I think that's how we are as people. I think we love people, down deep I really do. I think we love them so much that we are willing to carry them, but we also know that finding out how to do things yourself and winning on your own, even if that means losing yourself and learning from that, is a very important lesson. In its own way, even as a fun, up-tempo song, I think "AHBA" had a pretty real point of view.

IT WAS ONE OF THOSE SONGS THAT YOU JUST KEPT **PLAYING IN YOUR TRUCK.** - g

ONE NIGHT A DAY

BY GARY BURR AND PETE WASNER

G: Pete Wasner's a writer on this. He'd use Jack's Tracks to do demos and stuff—was around at the time. He also played, I think, on some of Kathy Mattea's stuff, was a player that Allen and Mark are both very comfortable having in this house. Great talent. In fact, it was Mark Miller who came up to me and said, "Hey man, there's a song you should hear." He'd never suggested anything up to that point. But he says it's called "One Night a Day," and, man, it was beautiful. It was sex on a record.

Allen Reynolds: To me, the song just felt like it was something Patsy Cline would have walked off with and done so perfect. It was big. Just a great fit for Garth.

G: You talk about Bobby Wood's wheelhouse, talk about Mike Chapman's wheelhouse. This is all the slinky, soulful, deepwater stuff that these guys grew up playing.

Bobby Wood: One of my favorites is "One Night a Day." It was really hard for me to play because the songwriter had, I don't know if he had played piano or what he played on it, but it wasn't easy to learn, I remember that. But I really liked what it was doing. Garth wanted kind of a clubby-type B3 organ on it, so I actually talked him into calling one of the Memphis guys, Bobby Emmons, to come in and play that. I said, "This guy is a real organ player." So Bobby came in and put B3 on. It's kind of a melodic, moody song, which is kind of my forte. A really soulful track.

Allen Reynolds: Another great player, Jim Horn, did the sax on that. Jim Horn is the boss on saxophone and other instruments. Played on so many recordings, with the Wrecking Crew, with guys from the Beatles, Clapton, and on and on. Later Garth called him up and asked him if he would teach him to play the solo so he could do it on his shows.

G: I knew we had a second television special coming up. I knew it was going to be on a large scale, whatever it was. I thought this was a chance for me to get to branch out, you know, me playing the sax in front of these people in the stadium. What a stupid idea that was. *(laughs)* Because saxophone isn't just putting your fingers on frets and all the sudden, if it's tuned good, it's going to be okay. Sax is a constant muscle of keeping that thing in key and, *Oh, my God*, soul. That would be nice to have … but did I think of that? So the squarest, whitest guy on the planet is getting ready to pick up one of the most soulful, sexiest instruments God ever created, and he's going to try to play it in front of 68,000 people in a Texas Stadium, standing on a piano while being filmed doing it … whose idea was this?

I love the fact that our crowds, that with them you could try it on. Forgiving people. The first time I tried was in the Tacoma Dome, and they were so sweet to me, you know, but it was absolutely … it was not good. They got more than they wanted, it was a buffet and the price was cheap. I got all the humility I wanted on that night, I can tell you that, for sure.

THEY GOT MORE THAN THEY WANTED, IT WAS A BUFFET AND THE PRICE WAS CHEAP. **I GOT ALL THE HUMILITY I WANTED ON THAT NIGHT.** - g

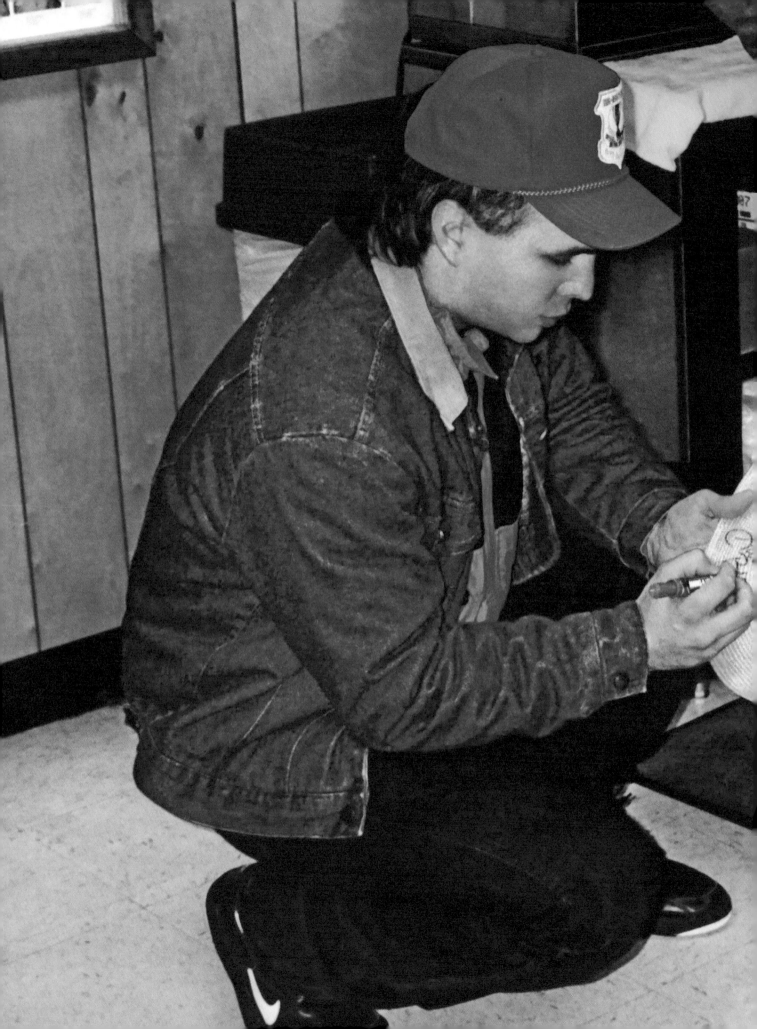

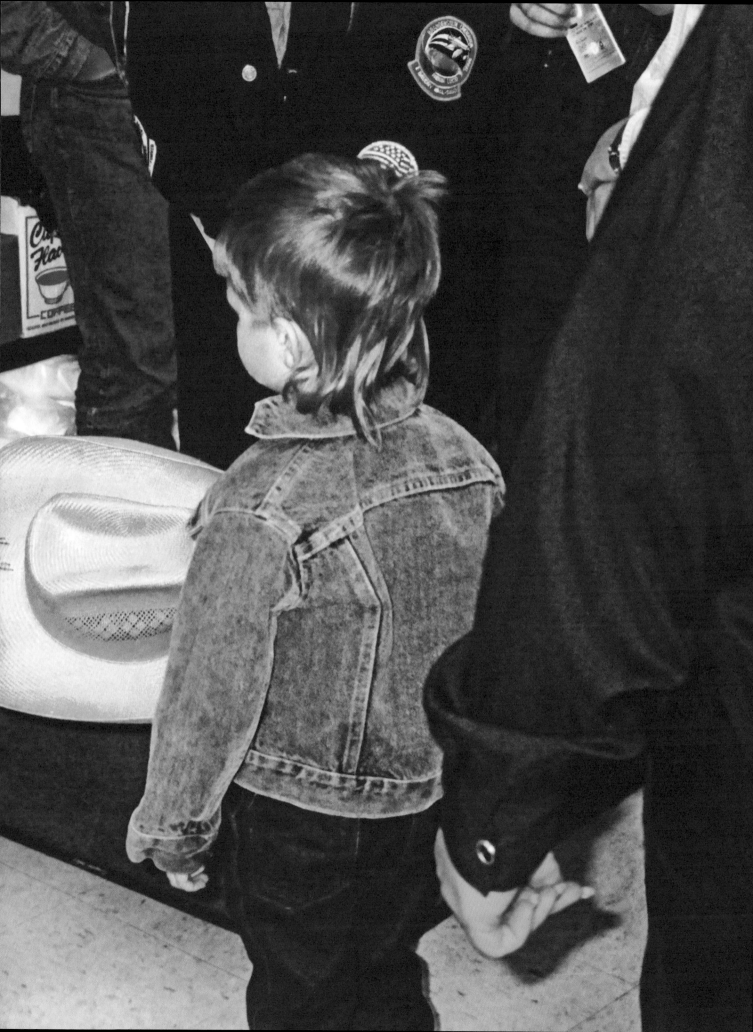

NASHVILLE NUMBER SYSTEM

EVEN WHEN WE had demos for songs we were going to cut, Allen would want me to go out into the studio and play the song for the musicians, you know, just me and guitar, rather than play them the demo. A demo could be filled with ideas about how the song should be played, and Allen wanted us to open things up as wide as we could. So he needed them to hear a song in its simplest forms, leaving the players as much space as possible to imagine the possibilities. In a bunch of cases, what we cut was very, very different from the demo of the song. Even as I played the song down for the guys, one of them would act as leader and chart the song using the Nashville System. And I'm telling you, every single one of those musicians could chart a song. Milton Sledge could chart the song, and a lot of people think a drummer not only wouldn't need that but couldn't *do* it. But damn, he could, and he could add in passing chords or whatever else was called for.

This way of writing charts is another of those Nashville things. All the Nashville players can chart songs this way, and it's geared toward recording. Since it's a number system, it allows singers to change keys if they need to, without the charts having to be changed. Changing keys using standard notation would be a huge ordeal. They came up with the Nashville Number System in the 1950s, and it just became a part of life.

I think we still have most of the charts from the recording sessions. You know, these charts and the track sheets, they're these cool artifacts, traces of what happened on those days we were working with Allen. Just looking at them, so much comes back to me. I remember Mike Chapman, the bass player and a guy who … I mean, he played on every record, he was writing a chart for one of the songs, and just by writing it out on paper, he could appreciate what it was doing musically. I can still see his face, he looked up and said, "Yeah, that's cool." And I knew right then we were swimming in deep waters, these musicians saw music everywhere and lived it through and through. What a feeling.

KICKIN' AND SCREAMIN'

BY TONY ARATA

Tony Arata: I wrote that song down in St. Augustine, Florida. I always write when I come down here and just walk up and down the beach. I don't bother anybody, and you take all the time you want to write a song.

G: "Kickin' and Screamin' " was just so much fun, and it was a side of Tony Arata that hadn't been shown in our stuff yet. This isn't "The Dance" or "Face to Face." It's something else, but he still goes after a big theme. He ties the circle of life in here, you know, telling us however you go out—you're going to go out—it'll be the same way you came in, kicking and screaming. You live your whole life kicking and screaming. What I love is this idea that, for all the changes, you never really grow up. You're just making noise, making sure everyone knows you're on this planet, trying to leave a mark with how much you're kicking the ground.

Tony Arata: I grew up in a big, big family. And the get-togethers, well, they were a bit nerve-wracking. I had a couple of uncles that always made things a little dicey, like you were always walking around wondering when the other shoe was gonna drop and the fights were gonna start. That's really something I'd never so much told to someone else, and the song gave it a place. So the first verse is about that. But then it's like, where are you gonna go from here? Somehow, it got to the hanging.

G: That's how it was for everybody who grew up in that era. You so enjoyed seeing your cousins, but you knew it was going to end bad every time. Tony made light of it, which I really enjoyed. But then it went wider, every verse taking it to a new place.

Tony Arata: I had gotten a little copywriting business going. I was writing stuff for manuals and things like that. Not what I thought of as my life's work. That's when I got a call saying that they wanted to do this song. And nobody else had ever had it on hold, I'm sure. But there again, Garth was different. He saw it as something that filled a slot on this record, and, man, the fat-cat musicians that he always recorded with, they just turned it into a real rockin' number.

G: *In Pieces* was, more than any of those first albums, a live show. It'll wear you out. Even "Kickin' and Screamin' " is kind of taking a breath, even though this is more of an upbeat thing. For that band, it was just free time, recess. My vocal could go somewhere it never got to go, that growl. We were all kind of playing in a new part of the playground. It was one of those gems that made a nice little place for itself on the album.

IN PIECES WAS, MORE THAN ANY OF THOSE FIRST ALBUMS, **A LIVE SHOW.** - g

207

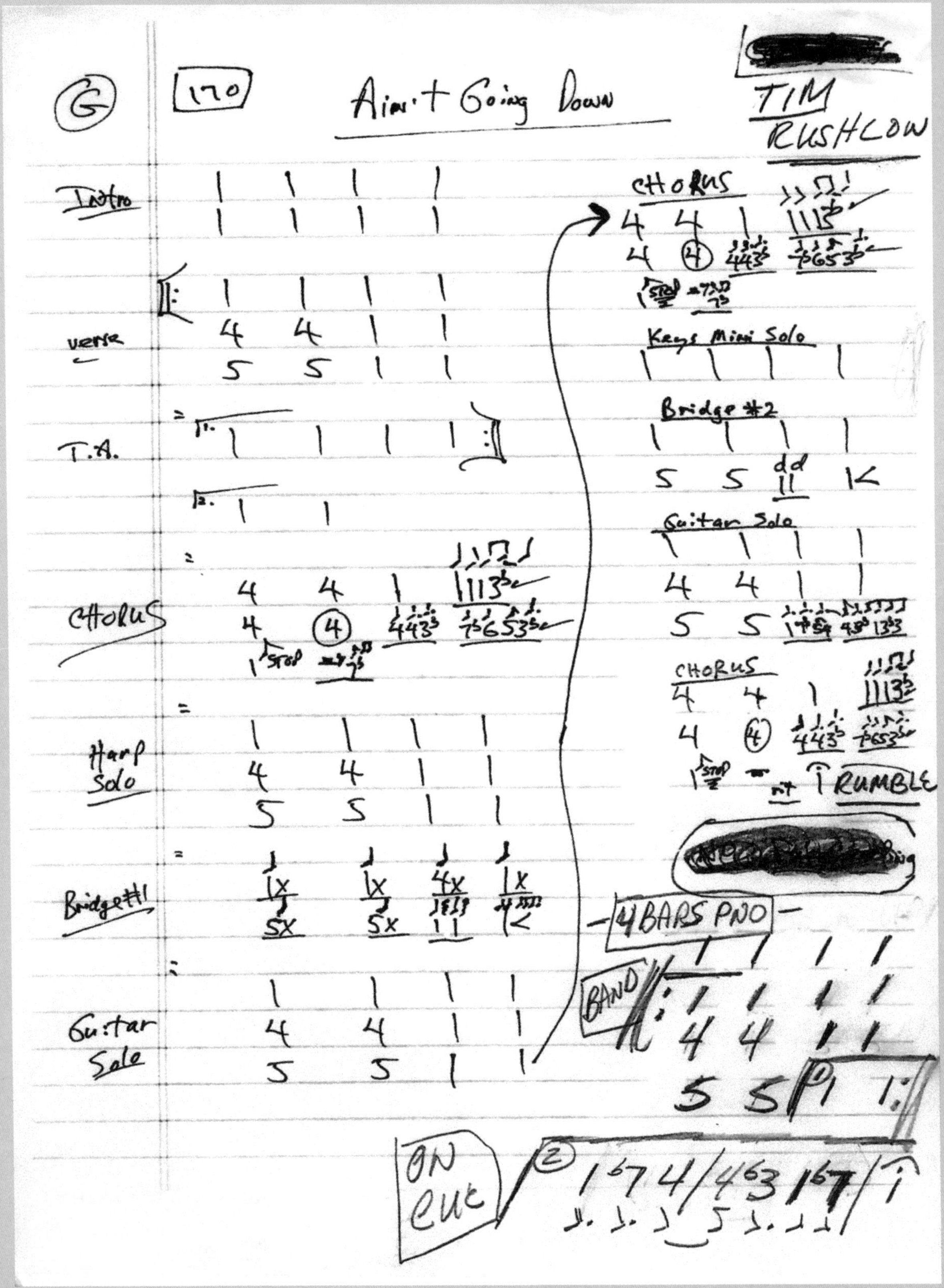
G
170
Ain't Going Down
TIM RUSHLOW
Intro
verse
T.A.
CHORUS
Harp Solo
Bridge #1
Guitar Solo
CHORUS
Keys Mini Solo
Bridge #2
Guitar Solo
CHORUS
STOP
rit
RUMBLE
4 BARS PNO
BAND
ON CUE

AIN'T GOIN' DOWN ('TIL THE SUN COMES UP)

BY KENT BLAZY, KIM WILLIAMS AND GARTH BROOKS

Bobby Wood: Well, that's definitely 300 miles per hour with your hair on fire.

Kent Blazy: I had just moved into another house that needed a whole lot of work, and Garth called me up around that time and said he wanted to write a song with machine gun lyrics, said, "Call Kim Williams." For me, whatever Garth said, I'm like, "Okay, whatever, machine gun lyrics sounds like fun to me." So I called Kim, and I said that Garth wants to write a song with machine gun lyrics. And Kim says, "What the hell does that mean?" *(laughs)* I said, "Does it matter? It's Garth." He's like, "No, you're right." So we got together, and because people were working on my house, banging, hammering, and painting and all that stuff, we went out on the back porch—out into the sunshine—and wrote machine gun lyrics all day.

G: It's hot outside, but we have to go outside because you can't hear yourself think with all the work going on. Out on the porch, Kim is sweating like an Eskimo in July—it's pouring out of him. Kent, who gets along with a fence post—like, I've never seen him complain about anything—he's in there just chugging away, and we are laughing so hard, just trying to squeeze as many syllables into each line as we possibly can. And there's no place to breathe with so many words, so all Kim keeps

GARTH CALLED ME UP AROUND THAT TIME AND SAID HE WANTED TO WRITE **A SONG WITH MACHINE GUN LYRICS.**

- KENT BLAZY

saying is, "How you gonna do this live, you can't breathe, you can't breathe." I'm like, "We'll figure that when we get there." What we didn't know as we were doing it was that the lyric was becoming the cadence of the song, it was becoming the rhythm of the thing, the beat. You know, "You better get your red head back in bed before the morning," that red head becomes a push in the song, and it's funny because the whole studio band picked up on that immediately, that the lyric was the cadence, and they followed that cadence through it all.

Kent Blazy: Finally, when we were all sunburned, we decided it was all done, and Garth wanted to make a little work tape of it. So my studio wasn't all together yet, but I had enough that I could do a little work tape with a drum machine on it. Back then drum machines were terrible, and especially if it was a guitar player programming it, because it sounded like a guitar player was playing drums. Garth and Kim were standing behind me while I was working the controls, getting everything together, and one of them says, "Oh, my God!" I turned around and there were *termites* coming out of the wall and the floor and ceiling.

Now, this was my new house, and I had a termite letter that said there were no termites, but the drum machine is pissing them off or something. I was kind of freaking out, because it's my new house and it's got termites. Kim Williams, just to show his sense of humor, he goes, "Oh man, don't worry about it, when Garth and I wrote 'Papa Loved Mama,' there were cockroaches crawling all over my apartment, and it was a number one song. So this is going to be one, too." Turns out he was right.

Allen Reynolds: That was so much fun to cut. With "Ain't Goin' Down" his breath control is so impressive. Just try singing the lines on that song without taking a breath, try and I bet you can't do it.

G: We brought in Terry McMillan, and this guy was crazy great, his harmonica playing was like no other. And on this track, he got to

Garth and Kent Blazy.

Trisha Yearwood: My biggest memory of "Ain't Goin' Down" is that there's a melody in that, this lick, where he's singing, and in my head I see it like the rise when you're on the roller coaster and you're getting ready to just go straight up to the top for that first dive. That's how I feel when I'm singing it. It just keeps going and going and going, and it was really hard, because it's not like you're going from note to note, you're sliding, so my slide has to match his slide or it sounds off. We got it, but it always bugged me, because I always felt like it was flat at the top. I always felt like my harmony wasn't perfect. Garth just thought the thing had the right feel. So, like twenty-five years later, when Garth remixed and remastered these albums, I said, "I want to listen to that." I said, "*I want to fix it.*" He said, "Yeah, you can fix it, but I'm telling you, it's on." So we broke it down, just playing the voices. He was right. *(laughs)* Twenty-five years later, I'm finally okay with it.

do every lick he's ever known. I remember Chris Leuzinger hearing that harmonica, and Chris has already put his guitar on, and going, "Oh, hell no." Chris rebooked his session, came in with his Marshall amps. He'd never brought his Marshalls to a session. Lined them up against the back wall here in the drum booth, kept the door open, stood about five feet out from the drum booth, and he would not sit down, just played this entire song, solos and all, standing up, competing with that brilliant stuff McMillan was doing. They went at it. He said, "That's the only way he's going to compete on this one." I thought it showed up great on the record. The fade on this thing is easily thirty to forty-five seconds, and after Allen did the fade and sent it to the label, they asked for a shorter one for radio. He said, "You betcha, I'll get you a shorter one, but I'm telling you right now, they won't play the shorter one." And I'll be damned, still to this day, when you hear it on the radio, they play the entire fade because of the performance from those two guys, Chris and Terry, back and forth.

G: I really think about every song on every album, and I started not feeling sure about this one. Just for a second. But after Trisha Yearwood came in and sang on it, she went back to Garth Fundis, her producer, and told him she just sang on the record that she wants to find for herself. *That* gave me all the confidence in the world to go in and finish the song up and expect it to do the big things that it did.

"MOMMA'S ON THE FRONT PORCH **SCREAMIN' OUT HER WARNING** GIRL YOU BETTER GET YOUR RED HEAD BACK IN BED BEFORE THE MORNING"

Left to right: Garth, Kent Blazy, and Kim Williams.

THE RED STROKES

BY JAMES GARVER, LISA SANDERSON, JENNY YATES AND GARTH BROOKS

Jenny Yates and Garth.

Allen Reynolds: I remember one time Jimmy Bowen said to me, "I bet it's something being in the studio with that energy." I told him, "Yeah, it really is." But his eyes were big as he was saying it, like, *Boy, I really bet it's something being around that.* But think about it, Bowen was a producer, Sinatra's producer. I mean, he was more than that, but as a producer of an artist working at the highest level, he knew enough to know I was dealing with something special, with a very passionate, driven artist. A producer's dream.

Bob Doyle: Garth is either on 110 percent, or he'll fall asleep, just like that. He can turn it off when he's done with whatever he's doing and needs to recharge. It's fascinating. Most of us will lie down, thinking and thinking. He shuts it off somehow, and then, once he's back engaged, it's at 110 percent, again. Remarkable energy, remarkable passion.

Trisha Yearwood: Garth is that guy that … let's say you're sitting in a room and having dinner with friends, and there's one guy at the table who's recently been divorced but nobody's talking about it; Garth is the one at the table that's gonna go, "So, man, are you okay?" You know, in front of everybody, "Are you okay, how are the kids?" And everybody else at the table, for a moment, is going to think, *Maybe he shouldn't be bringing that up.* And then the guy is like, "Well, yeah, everything is okay, I guess." And then this dinner table conversation becomes something more, some-thing deeper than, you know, "Who do you think is going to win the Stanley Cup?" It becomes a deeper conversation because he's not afraid to ask the questions that some-times make us a little uncomfortable, questions about relationships, life, families. I think at this point people have come to expect that, well, we're not really sure what we're going to get with this guy, but we know it will be real.

G: This song started with the thought of a painting and life's colors, the idea of represent-ing the passions, the energies, all these things that we want in our lives, but as the canvas becomes life and as the canvas becomes love, the red strokes are the ones. The picture they're painting in the song is one of the heart, and these two see it's a true work of art.

Jenny Yates: Garth picked up his guitar and played me what he had of "The Red Strokes." He had a good "map" for me to jump into.

THESE AREN'T CONTRADICTIONS— THE THUNDER AND THE VELVET— JUST TWWO SIDES OF A THING, **TWO SIDES OF A PASSIONATE LIFE.** - g

G: I liked the idea and loved the line "thundering moments of tenderness rage." It reminded me of a Dan Fogelberg song, a song called "Leader of the Band," where he talks about his dad, a "thundering velvet hand." It's the idea that these aren't contradictions—the thunder and the velvet—just two sides of a thing, kind of two sides of a passion-ate life. And those thundering moments of tenderness, rage—again, man, it's also just another beautiful way to talk about my favorite subject to sing about, and that is passion. A song like this is one of those pictures that you get to paint as a songwriter. I'm getting to use words to talk about oils and paints on a canvas, and about lives lived passionately. Music is the thing that gets there in the most satisfying way.

I love seeing a song's images, and the greatest songwriters, the ones I've admired the most, they have images so far out there, but when they hit me, I see exactly what they're talking about. How do they do that? It's deep communication, and one of the greatest communicators in the history of the planet, of mankind, has to be Bob Dylan. His simplicity, it's like a direct arrow from what he's thinking to your brain and heart, and that simplicity is where I see his genius. It's not about being above your head or impressing you with how smart he is. The real genius is in the simplicity. But you've got to be smart to do it. Simplicity, more than anything, paints those pictures that get you in the heart.

CALLIN' BATON ROUGE

BY DENNIS LINDE

Left to right: Jerry Douglas, Sam Bush, Garth, Béla Fleck, Pat Flynn, John Cowan, and second engineer Richard Aspinwall.

G: I found more out about the history of this song after we cut it, but I first heard the New Grass Revival version. They were on the same label, Capitol, and I heard that cut and just went, *Holy cow, that's a monster smash.* So I'm driving with one of the label's radio reps, one of the sales reps down in Dallas, and the song has just died in the thirties on the country charts, and I ask him, "What was up with that, why this song? How could you possibly lose that song?" He looks at me and says that songs with city titles in them never do good. *What?* "Kansas City," "City of New Orleans," "New York, New York." I'm sitting there thinking, *Are you fucking kidding me?* But what you find out in the record business is that there's a billion excuses for everything. It's just what the record business does. So I said, "That's bullshit, and if I get a chance I'm going to cut that. But I just want to cut it a little different."

Bob Doyle: It became just one of those moments in the studio, and what they did to make it work really translates ... I mean, this can be lifted from the studio and put into the concert hall and you feel all the same power, same excitement.

Allen Reynolds: New Grass Revival recorded that song, and Garth loved it, was just a huge fan of that group. So we cut the song, and then we brought New Grass Revival in to overdub on it. Sam Bush and Béla Fleck and Pat Flynn and John Cowan, with John Cowan singing the harmony, I think. Béla's a genius on banjo and Sam on mandolin and fiddle. They sat just perfectly on top of the track we'd recorded, just lifted it up.

G: When you start studying the song, you find that the songwriter, Dennis Linde, is a legend—you know, wrote "Burning Love" for Elvis, bunch of stuff. But the Oak Ridge Boys come out with it first, around ten years before the New Grass boys; they treated it as a kind of Cajun sing-along. New Grass brought in the bluegrass side of it. What we put into the mix was that hard-rock bottom end. Nobody had hit the Rockman on this thing, and it's going to grab your attention, grab you by the collar and shake the shit out of you the whole time you're singing it. We brought in our basic five guys, took Bobby off piano and put him on this low synth thing, and these guys cut it so low-end that they didn't even know what they were cutting. But we were laying down what we call "the carpet." They put a foundation down so thick, and then the call goes out to New Grass Revival.

Mark Miller: Sam Bush played the fiddle and mandolin, sang some harmony, just brilliant. John Cowan sang harmony and Béla Fleck played banjo. Pat Flynn on guitar. Jerry Douglas came along and played Dobro … He'll do in a pinch, right? *(laughs)* All these guys, just the best.

G: They'd been disbanded because they … well, maybe because they'd been in a band together, and if you think families are complicated, you should start your own band and see how that goes. But they got back together, brought Jerry Douglas with them, the world's greatest Dobro player. Mark Miller came in and used partitions to set this big room up, moved the piano out and set it up like a pie; it had five different slots, all looking at each other, and there they were, forced into one little room, all five of them, looking at each other, and now we're going to drop the flag and it's fricking game on. And here they went, Sam Bush, Cowan, all those guys. That's a memory I don't plan to trade for anything, ever.

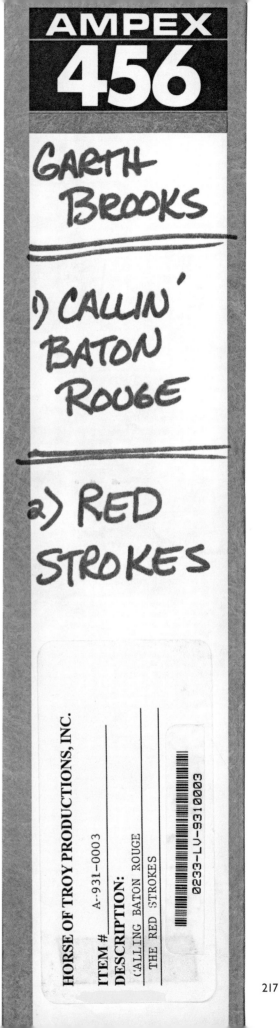

AMPEX
456

GARTH BROOKS

1) CALLIN' BATON ROUGE

2) RED STROKES

HORSE OF TROY PRODUCTIONS, INC.
ITEM # A-931-0003
DESCRIPTION:
CALLING BATON ROUGE
THE RED STROKES

0233-LV-9310003

THE NIGHT WILL ONLY KNOW

BY STEPHANIE DAVIS, JENNY YATES AND GARTH BROOKS

Stephanie Davis.

G: The original title was "That Summer Night in 1962." We have the demo, and the lyric is all different. It was kind of a movie idea, really cinematic, and I just loved working with it from the very beginning. You had two people that actually saw a murder happen, but they were both committing immoral crimes themselves, so they couldn't bear witness to the murder or their lives would have been affected as well. But in the first version, the crazy thing was that the murder they witnessed was Marilyn Monroe's.

Stephanie Davis: I would say he is a visionary, period. Even as you're writing, he's thinking about how this is going to fit on an album, how this is going to fit on the stage, what the video is going to look like. He's just got that kind of mind, and he sees the big picture, sees how it's going to go. Not me, I'm worried if *dime* rhymes with *time*, you know, I'm just back there scribbling.

Trisha Yearwood: I can see the movie and I can smell the sweat. It was like you really feel like you are in it, and that's the mark not just of great songwriting but of a great singer, one that pulls you in and makes you believe.

THAT'S THE MARK NOT JUST OF GREAT SONGWRITING **BUT OF A GREAT SINGER, ONE THAT PULLS YOU IN AND MAKES YOU BELIEVE.**
- TRISHA YEARWOOD

G: What a wicked, wicked web we were weaving with that song. The innuendos, the story. It also had a complicated rhyme scheme to it, really difficult to write. But it was a great challenge, and I just loved the way that it felt. With songs we have so much rewriting to do. They often start one place and end up in another, which happened with this one. We're not writers, we're *rewriters*. So you write the song, but then you spend a thousand times as long rewriting it, going back over it, making it smoother, making that corner a little nicer so it doesn't jolt you so much, or sharper where you *want* the jolt. You just rewrite, rewrite, rewrite. But in that process, you're also condensing, boiling the thing down to its essentials, just to get that entire story told in a short amount of time.

Jenny Yates: It was so visual. Hence we got into what is probably my favorite songwriting experience, which became "The Night Will Only Know." I recall that song taking a few months to write, and that means working on it every day, and it was wonderful. For me, the writing is the best part, the trying to find it, the *better-ing* it. Finishing and being proud of a song is great, but the getting there is everything, and this one kept us engaged in it for a good, long, wonderful while.

G: I graduated college because my dad said I had to get my degree. *(laughs)* I wanted to study music, but I couldn't read or write musical notation. So advertising made sense because it was a little like songwriting, you know, how much can you say in the shortest amount of time?

And that was a gift for me to learn how to condense in that way, to find the small detail that lets a person see a bigger scene. Man, it was a skill that fit right into creating songs like this one. And, for me, that night, that scene, will live forever—their first time to lie together. And the way the music builds the scene, like once the crime is committed, the police show up and that whole guitar solo that starts with that police siren, Leuzinger just paints it.

THE COWBOY SONG

BY ROY ROBINSON

G: The first time, the very first meeting with Bob Doyle at ASCAP, I go into his office and it's … well, it's an office in Nashville, and it's pretty cool just to be there. But we're sitting there, and he's asked to do something quickly and has to step out for two seconds. So I'm just walking around looking at plaques on the wall, pictures. On the corner of his desk is a cassette, and the cassette says "The Cowboy Song." When he comes back in, I go, "Hey, this tape, can I take it?" Because it's a cowboy song, and that's what I do. Bob said, Sure, and when I picked it up, the other side said, "Amos Staggs." Well, I fall in love with "The Cowboy Song" before I ever get a publishing or

TIME IS THE TRUE TEST OF SINCERITY. - g

writing deal…maybe 1987. It takes me five years to find the writer, Amos Staggs. Turns out, Amos Staggs was a stage name that this guy had, the writer's name was Roy Robinson, and it took me forever to locate him, find him out there in Texas. I sang that song for five years on my guitar, around campfires, wherever I was.

Chris Leuzinger: It's really rare that you find yourself on your fifth album with an artist. That's really rare in this business. You'd usually do two or three, *maybe* three, and they'd move on and get different musicians, a different producer, different this or different that. So with Garth, we're talking about the same band, same engineer, same producer. It just makes things happen that I don't think would normally happen. Five albums … and we weren't done.

Allen Reynolds: I felt like the songs led us to a great extent. Garth is very involved in the song selection, and song creation even. But when we get in here, it's also like the songs would lead us and we would try, in selecting the songs, to not repeat ourselves a lot. We've got this really interesting artist, and we're just trying to express all the sides and angles and edges of the artist. This studio was a refuge, and we were all here as friends to work on doing just that.

G: Roy Huskey Jr. came in and played standup bass, one of the most phenomenal standup bass players there are. He didn't do sessions anymore, but he was sweet enough to come in on this one. We had Bruce Bouton in to play steel, but we were feeling that the electronics of the steel just didn't seem to fit the acoustic version of this song. So he tells us he plays Dobro, and that's him playing Dobro, very simple, beautiful licks. It worked very well for this cut. There are no drums on this, I think it was just Roy Huskey Jr. kind of keeping the count on the bass, clicking.

After all the years I'd sat on this one, trying to find the writer, waiting for the song's moment, here it comes. There's a saying that I live by: "Time is a friend to all things good." Time is going to tell you whether something is going to stick around or not. Time is the true test of sincerity. It just is. I lived with this song, and finally the writer shows up, got to cut it, and this magic moment happens, and it's perfect for the end for what is probably the loudest record that you've ever had in your name, just to do an acoustic cowboy song on the way out. To nod to those cowboys, those men and women in the hats again, who showed up when no one else did, there's the tribute.

"SO WHEN YOU SEE THE COWBOY, HE'S NOT RAGGED BY HIS CHOICE HE NEVER MEANT TO BOW THEM LEGS OR PUT THAT GRAVEL IN HIS VOICE **HE'S JUST CHASIN' WHAT HE REALLY LOVES AND WHAT'S BURNIN' IN HIS SOUL"**

I GUESS YOU HAD TO BE THERE

BY BRYAN KENNEDY AND GARTH BROOKS

Bryan Kennedy: This one's from my first writing appointment with Garth. The song idea and the approach came fairly quickly.

G: For me, what makes a great story song is the imagery you can create as a songwriter, as the teller of the tale. And a great story song is usually told by someone who was there "as a witness" to whatever event and whatever people are being described. But when a story song is told in *first person*, well, now you're inside the skin of the storyteller. Now it becomes the gospel.

Bob Doyle: He's a keen observer of people, and, as a writer, he's always trying to make his observations in a conversational style, but through compelling, emotive stories.

Trisha Yearwood: For me, what defines a classic country song is a well-told story that makes me feel something. And this song did it for me. But on top of that, it sounded like something Reba would have recorded. That made it all the better for me, because Reba was and still is the ultimate compliment to any country songwriter.

G: As with so many of my songs, the artist I saw in my head, that I was writing for, was always Reba or Strait. This song, even though we did both a male and a female demo version of the

> ## A GREAT STORY SONG IS USUALLY **TOLD BY SOMEONE WHO WAS THERE "AS A WITNESS."**
> \- g

song, was steered by my thinking about Reba and her vocal prowess.

Bryan Kennedy: We did the demo over at Welk Studios, and Garth kept telling me about a girl he knew that just had to sing this song. I was good with that, even though I'd never heard of her. When we got to the moment for cutting "I Guess You Had to Be There" in the session, this girl went out to the vocal booth and began her "scratch" vocal. My God . . . Hello, *Trisha Yearwood*!

G: "I Guess You Had To Be There" was my first songwriting effort with Trisha's voice on it, the first of *many* to come.

WHICH ONE OF THEM

BY GARTH BROOKS

G: This is one of the three songs I brought to Nashville with me. It was written when I was playing with the Skinners in a band called Santa Fe. We were playing the Silver Dollar Ballroom outside of Stillwater, Oklahoma. I had just finished writing it, and there was a spot in the show that called for a slow dance. I asked Tom Skinner if I could try out a new song, just me and guitar. I remember standing up there, kind of wondering how this would go . . . and no one left the dance floor, they just stayed out there. They all slow danced like they did to the songs they were familiar with. It was a great feeling.

Bob Doyle: "Which One of Them" was one of those great honky-tonk barroom ballads. Like those classic George Jones ballads, it was very direct and to the point. I was drawn to the song by the melody and Garth's sincerity in telling the story. The performance was so believable.

G: It was originally written for Reba to sing, because I always thought "Which One of Them" was a classic female country song. The verses sound like something a female artist would sing, but I was never sure if a woman would sing the chorus. Songs are like that, you get what you get and sometimes you don't know what to do with it. Bob heard it immediately and connected with it.

Bob Doyle: I think most of us have had those moments in relationships, where we don't quite know what to do, and some of our short-term solutions don't solve anything.

I REMEMBER STANDING UP THERE, KIND OF WONDERING HOW THIS WOULD GO . . . AND **NO ONE LEFT THE DANCE FLOOR, THEY JUST STAYED OUT THERE.** - g

LEON

BY BUDDY MONDLOCK AND GARTH BROOKS

IT'S WHAT MUSIC AND SONGWRITING ARE ALL ABOUT. NO BIG COMMERCIAL IDEA, NO BIG PRODUCTION, JUST HEART AND SOUL, RECORDED BARE AND SIMPLE . . . THE TRUTH.

- g

G: As a song, "Leon" is the epitome of innocence. And for me, it's what music and songwriting are all about. No big commercial idea, no big production, just heart and soul, recorded bare and simple … *the truth.* Charlie was a friend of mine who worked all day at a gas station, took care of his wife and children, and was always there for you when you needed someone. Leon was his son and nothing but love, a happy child, and all boy.

Buddy Mondlock: Garth said he wanted to write about Charlie but to address the song to Leon. He already had the first few lines in his head, and the song almost wrote itself. That's how you know you're on to something good! It was just a true feeling about a really good guy. Addressing it to his son was the door we needed to open to be able to see the rest of the song. Once we got that, it just came.

G: Even though this was just a demo, the *recording* of "Leon" amazes me. Like "The Cowboy Song," the stark quality speaks volumes. The sparse instrumentation leaves a path a mile wide for the lyric. The imagery is so clear you can see it. And that's Buddy Mondlock, an amazing talent.

Buddy Mondlock: Miles Wilkinson was the engineer. Garth played guitar and sang it live in the studio. Bruce Bouton overdubbed a little Dobro, and I added the harmony parts. I've always had a soft spot for this song and the recording we did of it … it was just simple and true. And that's what country music is all about.

TOMORROW AND TODAY

BY JOEL NASPINSKI, RANDY TAYLOR AND GARTH BROOKS

> ## I REMEMBER BEING A LITTLE UNCOMFORTABLE WRITING IT, **JUST BECAUSE IT WAS OUT OF MY COMFORT ZONE.**
>
> **- RANDY TAYLOR**

G: This is college. I'm playing around Stillwater, Oklahoma, at different clubs and coffeehouses. One of the people who showed up a lot was a kid going through school while working at the campus fire station. Joel was from Pennsylvania, and he was enamored with how the writing process worked. I told him Randy Taylor and I were getting together to write and he should just come over and write with us.

Randy Taylor: This may have been the last song we wrote before Garth left for Nashville. It's definitely from toward the end of the Stillwater days. I remember being a little uncomfortable writing it, just because it was out of my comfort zone. Garth went off into all these poetic images, and I'm the literal, sarcastic SOB.

G: I remember sitting around with no idea. But I love playing descending lines on the guitar, so as we're waiting for the idea to show itself, I'm playing this descending line over and over and over. The thought turns to *seasons* and how the seasons bring on a change. But if you're hurting from a relationship, one of those relationships that haunts you, it feels like change never happens to you. So, there was the idea, going through the seasons with no change.

Randy Taylor: I think it's the sweetest melody of anything we've ever written together.

G: This song still makes me smile. I can listen to it over and over, even after all this time.

LIKE WE NEVER HAD A BROKEN HEART

BY PAT ALGER AND GARTH BROOKS

Pat Alger: I had just gone through a painful divorce. Of course, is there any other kind? I was trying to date a little bit, and this title just came to me after one of those sad nights. I showed it to Garth, and I think he suggested we do it from the woman's point of view, which—in my opinion—gives the idea its power.

G: When Pat brought up the general idea of "Like We Never Had a Broken Heart," I didn't feel I had the guts *or* the courage to be that honest. As a guy, I find it hard enough to be the loser at love, let alone admit it and sing about it.

Pat Alger: The challenge was to make it as simple as possible and, at the same time, make it a strong statement for one lover to say to another in what's really a very vulnerable situation.

Trisha Yearwood: Back then, I could sometimes be more honest in a song than I could in a conversation or a relationship. And I thought this song was incredibly honest, and at a time when I wasn't ready to be that honest in life. For me, that was a really powerful experience.

G: I knew I would never make this statement as an artist, and so did Pat. I believe that's why we focused on a female voice being the driving force behind this song.

Trisha Yearwood: I sang the demo for this song, and I sang it every time Pat Alger had a writer's night at Douglas Corner. The lyrics were brutally honest, and the melody haunted me. By that time, I'd already decided that if I ever got a record deal, I was going to record it.

THE LYRICS WERE BRUTALLY HONEST, AND **THE MELODY HAUNTED ME.**

- TRISHA YEARWOOD

Pat Alger: For me, "Like We Never Had a Broken Heart" is what songwriting is all about. We didn't write it for a particular artist. We didn't write it to fit in with some current fad that songwriting was going through at the time. We wrote it for the song.

ONLY THE BEGINNING ...

EARLY SPRING, 1995. It's late. The bus is rolling back to Nashville. Everyone is asleep except for Bob Doyle and me ... and, we're hoping, the driver! We've just been to the manufacturing plant in Illinois, where Capitol Records has awarded us with the Fifty Million Record Sales party. Bob and I are sitting there, just digesting it all. There's a silence.

Then Bob asks, "How far do you think it can go?" In my head, I can hear Charles Koppelman, who ran EMI at the time, talking earlier that day about us hitting that sales mark, saying, "No one has done it faster." Bob had always said if we take care of the music, the rest would take care of itself. There on that bus, in the quiet, I told Bob, "Well, we're at fifty, and it's halfway through the decade, maybe if we take care of the music and the people, we could be at a hundred million by the end of the decade ... I don't think that's impossible." That scene sticks with me, because it reminds me just how much we believed in what we were doing. How much we believed in the people and in the music. And how much we believed that the first five years were only the beginning.

ACKNOWLEDGMENTS

The Garth Brooks Team would like to thank the following but not limited to: the Academy of Country Music, Alfred Music, Pat Alger, Matt Allen, Kheli Baucom, Randy Bernard, Kent Blazy, The Blazy Family, Anka Brazzell, The Brooks Family, Stephanie Brown, Don Cobb, Tommy Colorigh, Erin Conn, Cowtown Boots, Tina Crawford, Jeff Crump, Stephanie Davis, Bob Doyle, Michael Doyle, The England Family, Andy Friday, Charles Green, Beth Gwinn, Cheryl Harris, Luellyn Latocki Hensley, Dan Johnson, Rusty Jones, Jerry Joyner, Bryan Kennedy, Chris Leuzinger, Pam Lewis, Mark Miller, Buddy Mondlock, Craig Owens, Pat Quigley, Terry Palmer, Jeff Penick, Sam Powers, PRG Lighting, Kevin Pryzbylowski, Steve Puntolillo, Allen Reynolds, Nancy Seltzer, Theresa Smith, Randy Taylor, Virginia Team, Tami Thompson, Ticketmaster, Phyllis Williams, Bobby Wood, Trisha Yearwood, and Wendi Crosby York.

...and mostly to God, for it is through Him all things are possible.

PHOTOGRAPHY AND MUSIC

Photography:

Academy of Country Music, Nubar Alexanian, Allentown Studio Collection, Sharon Blazy, Garth Brooks' Family Collection, the Stephanie Davis Collection, Henry Diltz, Sonja England, Beth Gwinn, Philip Hight, Robert Spencer Ingman, Mike Jones, Lewis Lee, Pam Lewis, Richard Mackson/Getty Images, Alan Mayor, John Lee Montgomery, Natasha Moustache, Bev Parker, Don Putnam, Charley Stefl's Family Collection, Tami Rose Thompson, Kim Williams, and the Bobby Wood's Family Collection.

Sheet Music and Lyrics:

CREDITS

Produced by:

 **MELCHER MEDIA**

President, CEO: Charles Melcher
VP, COO: Bonnie Eldon
Executive Editor/Producer: Lauren Nathan
Production Director: Susan Lynch
Editor/Producer: Josh Raab
Senior Digital Producer: Shannon Fanuko
Assistant Editor/Producer: Karl Daum

Melcher Media would like to thank Callie Barlow, Jess Bass, Emma Blackwood, Renee Bollier, Amelie Cherlin, Barbara Gogan, Ashley Gould, Luke Jarvis, Emily Kao, Aaron Kenedi, Samantha Klein, Karolina Manko, Emma McIntosh, Jordie Oetken, Gabrielle Sirkin, Victoria Spencer, Megan Worman, Grace Yoon, Katy Yudin, Gabe Zetter, and Drea Zlanabitnig.

A VICTIM OF THE GAME

IT TOOK A LITTLE TIME BUT I GUESS YOU FINALLY LEARNED
PROMISES GET BROKEN BRIDGES DO GET BURNED
YOU'VE BEEN SIFTIN' THROUGH THE ASHES SEARCHIN' FOR THE FLAME
HOLDIN' ON TO NOTHING LIKE A VICTIM OF THE GAME

YOU WERE STANDIN' WAY TOO CLOSE TO SEE IT FALL APART
THERE WERE WORDS YOU COULDN'T HEAR LISTENIN' WITH YOUR HEART
YOU CAN'T SAY I DIDN'T WARN YOU THERE'S NO ONE ELSE TO BLAME
YOU'RE JUST THE LAST TO KNOW THAT YOU'RE A VICTIM OF THE GAME
                                        AS

IT DON'T MATTER WHO YOU ARE
IT TREATS EVERYONE THE SAME
ALL YOU NEED IS A HEART
TO BE A VICTIM OF THE GAME

When I look into your eyes ~~I~~ I can feel the pai

NOW I SEE YOU IN THE MIRROR AND I SWEAR YOU LOOK THE SAME
BUT I CAN'T AVOID THE EYES OF A VICTIM OF THE GAME
Staring in the mirror at a victim of the game
WHEN I SEE YOU IN THE MIRROR I WANNA LOOK THE OTHER WAY

But there's none quite as blind

BY: MARK D. SAND
COWBOY GART

really

racks RECORDING STUDIO INCORPORATED   1308 16th Ave. So., Nashville, Tennessee 37212– (615) 385-2555

TAPE TYPE: AMPEX 456
LEVEL: +5/200
SPEED: 30 IPS

NOTES Chris Leuzinger   3000 x
Milton Sledge   Mark Casstevens
Mike Chapman   Rob Hajacos

DATE	STUDIO	ENGINEER	REEL #	PURCHASE ORDER #															NOTES			
TUES PM		MARK MILLER																				

	8	9	10	11	12	13	14	15	16	17	18	19	20	21	22	23
						REMARKS		FAVOR MIC 4/6	4/6				SEE BACK 4/17			
										FIDDLE	CHRIS ELEC 4/4/40	VOC	VOC	VOC		ACOUST
NDS IN LOW PLACES	GROUP mic 4/13	GROUP BRINGIN 4/13	ELECTRIC		PIANO		STEEL DIR,	MIC 1 RePate BRUCE		Rob		MAIN		1ST US		
ON 2ND REPEAT			I 58	107/117	125/135	143→153	201→210	218/228	237/246	255/304	312/322	331/339	348/357	405/414	423/432	4

	7	8	9	10	11	12	13	14	15	16	17	18	19	20	21
								REMARKS						BGV.	VOC
OLVES	EDGAR MEYER BOWED BASS w/ch.2	JELLY RILL HARMONICA	DOBRO DIXE PIERCE		ELECTRIC		KEYS 4/40		KEYBOARD	ACOUSTIC		GROUP		INDIAN RIVER	